CW00362244

REDISCOVERING THE CHRIST

John R. Yungblut

ELEMENT

Rockport, Massachusetts • Shaftesbury, Dorset

© 1974 John R. Yungblut

Published in the U.S.A. in 1991 by
Element, Inc.
42 Broadway, Rockport, MA 01966

Published in Great Britain in 1991 by
Element Books Limited
Longmead, Shaftesbury, Dorset

All rights reserved.
No part of this book may be reproduced or utilized in any form or
by any means, electronic or mechanical, without permission in
writing from the Publisher.

Cover design by Max Fairbrother

Cover illustration by Giotto, courtesy of SCALA

Printed and bound in the U.S.A. by
Edwards Brothers, Inc.

Library of Congress Catalog Card Number available
ISBN 1–85230–266–6

Preface

In this book, I am addressing a broad but very specific audience. It contains members of three different groups: Christians, humanists, and devotees of the other living religions.

I hope, first of all, to speak to those questioning Christians who are no longer able to integrate into their worldview some aspects of the traditional concept of Jesus as the Christ, described by the creeds and doctrines of the Church. This concept includes such doctrines as the virgin birth, two separate and distinct natures in Jesus (the divine and the human), the bodily resurrection of Jesus, and an anticipated second coming.

Perhaps you are one of these questioning Christians. It is not that God is dead for you. He is still very much alive, and you feel impelled to bring your life into conformity with what you understand to be his will. But the image of the Christ no longer comes alive for you in those familiar terms in which it continues to be presented by the Church with reference to Jesus of Nazareth.

The Christ identified solely as Jesus may be said to be dead for you. And you may be feeling a sense of guilt about it, conscious or unconscious, suspecting that it may be your own fault, that it may represent lack of faith on your part. You may also be experiencing a poignant nostalgia, a sense of profound loss, almost an inward mourning for one you had loved long since and lost a while.

Because you can no longer conscientiously profess Jesus

as the Christ in the way you feel the Church still requires,
you may have abandoned as well your own private quest
of the historical Jesus in the New Testament. You may
have assumed that Jesus and this traditional Christ concept are inseparably one, as you have always been taught
by the Church, and you may find yourself turning sadly
away from the Jesus of history who has thereby lost his
charisma and urgent significance for you.

Since at an earlier period of my own pilgrimage I
should have counted myself one of you, I have no difficulty in identifying with you. If this is where you are, I
believe I understand what you are experiencing. And,
anticipating what I hope to share with you in this book, I
want first of all to reassure and to commend you for the
troubled state in which you find yourself. I think it is good
evidence of the integrity of your quest and of your continued growth in the life of the spirit.

The very meaning of the word "religion" springs from
its derivation from the Latin verb *religio* which is literally
translated "to bind into one bundle." Your instinctive in-
clination to reject beliefs that cannot be bound into one
bundle, made one harmonious whole, is to be trusted
implicitly as the most profound "religious" motivation. It
is the God-implanted drive in you "to get it all together."
Reason is not the only source of our knowledge. We have
ways of knowing intuitively and existentially that sup-
plement the faculty of reason.

But reason still is king. Any hypothesis which the mind
cannot plausibly put together in one world-view with new
and incontrovertible data must be forgone, no matter how
revered the hypothesis has become nor how traumatic the
initial parting must be.

But I have the temerity to hope for still more. If your
basic difficulties in embracing the ancient credo are akin
to what mine have been, and I suspect they may be, then
I believe that the line of argument I shall develop may

speak to your condition and come home to you with the impact of "good news." What I want to offer you, in terms I hope may be generally acceptable, is both motivation for returning as a disciple to the Jesus of history, and a new way of understanding the Christ which relates to Jesus and is at the same time necessarily distinguishable from him in very important respects. I want to share with you a way of looking at the Jesus of history and the Christ of faith that has gradually been taking shape in my thought and experience over the past four decades. I want to suggest how this perspective has enabled a great many things in our religious heritage and in our recently acquired knowledge about ourselves to interrelate and to "hang together" in a way that has continued to be exciting and convincing for me, and I trust may become so for some of you.

Moreover, it is not merely on the intellectual plane that I would speak to you. I am well aware that when I speak of Jesus and the Christ I touch the quick of your deepest religious sensibilities, even if some of these feelings have been long buried, consciously or unconsciously. I trust that, in proportion as you remain open to what I shall be trying to impart, I shall be reawakening in you stirrings of a sense of "the holy," aspirations long mistrusted and therefore neglected. But most of all I even hope to enter into communion with you on the deepest level of inspiration, giving rise to the infinite longing in which we may find that we are one with the Christ and with each other.

The second group I hope to address in this book is the humanists who dissociate themselves from any of the living religions in their institutional forms, but whose prevailing inward attitude is one of reverence toward man or toward a mysterious quality they persistently find in man.

Though members of no religious body, you are not strangers to the spirit of worship. You have found something in your own humanity and in that of others which elicits from you adoration, though you may not call this something "God." Unable to accept any of the historical revelations proclaimed by the various living religions, you are nevertheless looking in the right direction and in the right frame of mind for fresh revelation from the only source for it man has ever really known: the illimitable depths of his own being.

If you are this kind of humanist, I hope to persuade you to take a new look at your own experience and to see if it cannot be understood in the light of a concept of the Christ I shall present. I want to suggest that this something you already perceive in yourself and in other persons is in fact the Christ in a new sense you have never associated with the Church's teaching, a sense that may win your acceptance and even lead you to a profession of your own actual belief in God. Once again this will involve a clear distinction between this elusive, fluid, evolving Christ myth and the Jesus of history in whom, nevertheless, the Christ has been most vividly seen and known.

The third group with whom I would communicate is those devotees of other living religions for whom until now the Church's interpretation of Jesus as the Christ has been an insuperable barrier to genuine dialogue. Quite understandably your heritage is sacred to you, since it has formed the very marrow of your bones. You are not to be expected to embrace a radical discontinuity with all that has been precious, because indigenous, to you.

The Holy Spirit has not been without his witness at any time or at any place. As Arnold Toynbee has argued, that living religion will prove itself superior which shows itself capable of persuading devout members of *other* living religions that they can embrace its faith without forgoing anything in their own that has proved of abiding value. They will experience a progressive, inherent convergence of ideas and experiences that constitute one transparent, organic whole which is irresistible.

The coming world religion will not be a new, synthetic, eclectic amalgam, but such a continuing organic evolution of one of the existing religions as will prove itself capable of drawing circles large enough to take others in. Far from experiencing any threatening loss of identity, those who feel themselves so drawn will rejoice in a new sense of fulfillment. I should personally still hope that this "chosen" religion might be some form of Christianity, but I am certain it would have to be a form so expanded and universalized as to be quite transformed, while still recognizably belonging to the same historic phylum.

Obviously, the crux of any dialogue that would be more than mere clarification of differences with any of you who now belong to other living religions must take its point of departure from a new and universalized concept of the Christ. In presenting this concept to you, while not denying its historic association with the Jesus of history and the indelible stamp his person has imposed upon it, I want to demonstrate that the Christ myth has always had a life of its own. It has evolved from its inception in the "Messiah" concept of the Old Testament and is still evolving today.

You will recognize that it has had its counterparts in other religions and cultures, perhaps even your own. At all times and places there have been revelations, or at any rate intimations, whether acknowledged and recorded or not, of the nature of this universal manhood or of the emerging new man. But I am anticipating too much. I want just now only to suggest that in this book about Jesus and the Christ I hope to initiate with some of you a new level of dialogue.

Up to this point, this imagined audience I have been describing and hoping to assemble may seem too diverse and too vast to be credible. Let me now attempt to describe the particular characteristics which at once constitute a bond, however unrecognized, in the members of this audience, and also the basis of any exclusion, however undesired on my part.

I am well aware that the position I am about to present will speak to the condition only of those who have already been led, by whatever path, to perceive the world as one, a world in which everything is interpenetrated by everything else, a world in which there are no permanent dichotomies between natural and supernatural, matter and spirit, earth and heaven.

In other words, what I plan to say will be persuasive only to those who find themselves drawn to the mystical variety of religious experience as distinct from those varieties which would place the emphasis on the acceptance of credal formularies of historical revelations, on the authority of an infallible book or hierarchy, or on cultic liturgical practice. I believe that all men, by virtue of being human, possess a mystical faculty designed for the perception of interrelatedness. Only those who cherish this faculty as the growing edge of man's continuing evolution, and long for its ever greater development in themselves, will respond affirmatively to this contribution I propose to make to a new "Christology."

There is something else that has already conditioned this diverse, yet unitary, audience to whom I would speak. Only those will find themselves addressed and prepared to offer confirmation who have already assimilated into their world-view, at least to some extent, what I believe to be the two most distinctive perspectives acquired by modern man: the *evolutionary* and the *depth psychological*.

I must confess here that, next to brooding on the writings of the mystics, humanist as well as theist, the most important influences on the development of my own thought and experience have been the following: the study of the proofs of evolution in geology and paleontology as an undergraduate in college; the philosophical speculations to which this new knowledge gave rise in men like Bergson and Whitehead; the scientific and theological speculations of Lecomte du Nuoy and more recently Teilhard de Chardin; and finally, the reflections of Carl Jung on the meaning and value of the accumulating insights of depth psychology.

I know that evangelists like Billy Graham still list their conversions in a given mission in the hundreds or thousands. I confess to a haunting nostalgia and a seductive impulse to join the throng at the altar rail. I recognize that thousands are reached by attractive presentations of Jesus as the Christ who would be left cold by what I am writing here. I know too that storefront fundamentalist groups are growing proportionately faster than even the major denominations within Christianity.

Yet, with a certain sadness, I am aware that I cannot join these movements, even if I stand under their threat of damnation. I am forever incapable of bringing their version of Jesus as the Christ into synthesis with my worldview. However impressive their number counts, I am persuaded they represent the last convulsive movements of the will to live of a form of religious belief that is dying because it is no longer capable of integration with a worldview which, to me at least, clearly constitutes the wave of the future. True religion, as I understand it, levels upon me its imperious demand to "get it all together." So I turn reluctantly away from this orthodoxy and look for the narrow way that leads into life, in a direction not yet fully charted.

In this book I will first try to show in Chapter I how assimilation of the evolutionary and depth-psychological perspectives has meant for the "modern man" the death of the traditional Christ myth. Chapter II will undertake to sketch the varying forms of the Messiah myth with which Jesus was familiar and to inquire into his own quest of identity with reference to these. Chapter III will present the birth of the Christ myth in the Apostolic Church and its evolution within the New Testament writings. Chapter IV will attempt to demonstrate how the myth has continued to evolve throughout history, with reference to changing world-views. And the last chapter will present a remythologized form of the classic myth, which I believe to be viable within the world-view of modern man.

I do not claim any special originality for many of the insights gathered together here. Some of them were even entertained or foreshadowed by individual theologians of the early church who were adjudged heretics. Others have had their counterpart at various periods and places in the life of the Church until the present. One is never fully aware of the sources of his ideas, scrupulous as he may try to be. What is original here, as far as I am aware, is the way I have come to put these insights together into what I trust is a reasonably coherent whole. If another is thereby aided to arrive at his own interpretation of thought and feeling about Jesus and the Christ, this labor of love will be abundantly rewarded.

JOHN YUNGBLUT

April 1974
Pendle Hill
Wallingford, Pennsylvania

Contents

To my wife, June, who has helped me to understand the meaning and relevance of myth, and to Henry Cadbury, my teacher in New Testament at the Harvard Divinity School, who raised all the ultimate questions of Christology and steadfastly refused to answer any of them.

The substance of this book has been coming together in my mind over many years. During the final shaping of the thought, I had the benefit of dialogue with others during lecture series at the Earlham School of Religion in the winter of 1973, and at Pendle Hill in the winter of 1974.

I am grateful for the faithful and generous assistance of Barbara Harkins and Bonnie Favrot in preparing the manuscript, to Henry J. Cadbury and my colleague at Pendle Hill, Mary Morrison, for valuable critical suggestions, and to my editor, Michael Leach, for his patience and skill in helping to give it final form.

And, as always, I am grateful for the quiet and unflagging support of my wife, June.

I

Modern man and the death of the traditional christ myth

The beginning of our universe, if it can be said to have had a beginning, is shrouded in mystery, as is any conceivable end of it. But within the last century we have come to discover the startling nature of the evolutionary process that takes place on this planet in-between. The fact of our evolution may be, as Julian Huxley asserted, the most important discovery man has ever made.

Through this new lens, we have inherited a new way of looking at ourselves and our world that is at once inescapable and irreversible. From now on, we must think of ourselves within the context of biological space-time, or duration. Instead of being placed fully developed on the earth from above or beyond, we now know that we have sprung from the very bowels of the earth, children of matter.

At one stage of the earth's evolution, when the ecological conditions were just right, the phenomenon of cellular substance emerged from molecular substance, instituting the process of life, from which all existing forms of life on earth have emerged in due course. The process of creation, as far as life is concerned, has thereby been revealed as unfinished, continuing at this present moment and through the foreseeable future.

The New Perspectives of Our Time

Moreover, it is not as if we were talking about an unproved theory. We are speaking of a process which for all who have studied the evidence, past and present, with an open mind, recognize as incontrovertible fact. So vast and far-reaching are the implications of this master fact that we are compelled to rethink, with reference to it, all other theories or systems of knowledge, some of whose facticity we may have taken for granted until now. It is quite clear that modern Christians must reexamine and restate, for example, every theological doctrine: creation, original sin, incarnation, atonement, resurrection, and the second coming in the new light of the fact of evolution. Teilhard de Chardin sketches for us the full scope of the revolution in man's thought occasioned by this discovery, scarcely more than a century old:

Blind indeed are those who do not see the sweep of a movement whose orbit infinitely transcends the natural sciences, and has successively invaded and conquered the surrounding territory—chemistry, physics, sociology and even mathematics and the history of religions. One after the other, all the fields of human knowledge have been shaken and carried away by the same under-water current in the direction of the study of some development. Is evolution a theory, a system or a hypothesis? It is much more: it is a general condition to which all theories, all hypotheses, all systems must bow and which they must satisfy henceforward if they are to be thinkable and true. Evolution is a light illuminating all facts, a curve that all lines must follow.[1]

It is my conviction that the lines of the Church's Christology have not yet begun to follow that curve, and it is my hope that this book may make some contribution to

[1] Teilhard de Chardin, *The Phenomenon of Man* (New York: Harper Torchbooks, 1959), pp. 217–218. Reprinted with permission.

that end. One way of pointing to the common bond I perceive in the three groups within the congregation this book would address would be to designate them modern men in the very special sense Teilhard carefully defines for us: therefore, I address it to that particular modern man whom Teilhard identifies for us:

What makes and classifies a "modern" man (and a whole host of our contemporaries is not yet "modern" in this sense) is having become capable of seeing in terms not of space and time alone, but also of duration, or—and it comes to the same thing—of biological space-time; and above all having become incapable of seeing anything otherwise—anything—*not even himself.*[2]

One may say this is the new lens which modern man must focus upon any idea he would examine in proper perspective. This includes his personal doctrine of man, his understanding of who and what he himself is as well as his ultimate response to the persistent question of Jesus of Nazareth: "But who do you say that I am?"

Another perspective we must take into account in reformulating our ultimate convictions is that of depth psychology. It represents an extension, in one sense, of the more inclusive evolutionary perspective in the direction of the study of man's psyche. Modern man is inescapably post-Freudian as well as post-Darwinian. It is the insights of Carl Jung, however, inspired initially by Sigmund Freud, but going far beyond him in their scope and significance, that can be particularly helpful to us in our response, as modern men, to the question raised by Jesus. Jung has insisted on the importance of this new perspective:

For more than fifty years we have known, or could have known, that there is an unconscious as a counterbalance to conscious-

2 *Ibid.*, p. 218.

ness. Medical psychology has furnished all the necessary empirical and experimental proof of this. There is an unconscious psychic reality which demonstrably influences consciousness and its contents. All this is known, but no practical conclusions have been drawn from it. We still go on thinking and acting as before, as if we were simplex and not duplex.[3]

The Church, generally, in its doctrine of man and its doctrine of Jesus as the Christ, has gone on "thinking and acting as before, as if we were simplex and not duplex"— without an unconscious affecting consciousness. But the person to whom this book is addressed finds himself no longer able to do so. This modern man, as Jung describes him, will already

. . . have set his hand, as it were, to a declaration of his own human dignity and taken the first steps toward the foundations of his own consciousness, that is, toward the unconscious, the only accessible source of religious experience.[4]

His personal answers to the ultimate questions of his own identity and significance, and of the identity and significance of Jesus of Nazareth, will have to harmonize with what he perceives and experiences to be this duplex, evolving, psyche of man.

I am persuaded that within the last decade or two the extension of these two related perspectives, at least in elementary form, has been very considerable throughout the world. Many of you into whose hands this book has fallen may not have studied in any formal way either evolution or depth psychology. But if you have absorbed, even on a subliminal level, some of the basic discoveries about man's heritage as an animal and his present endowment as a duplex being with some spiritual promise,

[3] Carl Jung, *The Undiscovered Self* (New York: A Mentor Book, New American Library, 1959), pp. 95–96.
[4] *Ibid.*, p. 101.

and those insights have begun to shape your thinking and to demand important readjustments, then this book is intended to speak to you with passion and urgency.

The Meaning of Religious Myth

One other important word must be said at the outset. It is not necessary that we see eye to eye. But if I am to communicate the message I would impart, it is necessary that we look in the same direction and at least generally from the same perspective. I shall try to avoid as much as possible technical theological terminology except where the classic words seem indicated. But there is one word I shall find indispensable, and I must try at the outset to make reasonably sure that you will understand the special sense in which I am using it. I shall be referring more or less constantly to the evolving Christ *myth*.

The 1960 edition of Webster's Dictionary offers three definitions of the word "myth": "a legend; poetic fiction; a fabulous narrative founded on some event, especially in the early existence of a people, and embodying their ideas as to their origin, their gods, natural phenomena, etc." I shall be using the word in the last sense.

When I speak of the Christ myth I shall mean neither legend nor poetic fiction, but a fabulous narrative embodying deeper realities and profound truths. And I shall be referring to the Church's answer to Jesus' question as to who he was in its doctrine of Jesus as the Christ. This doctrine is a myth in the sense that it is "a fabulous narrative founded on some event (the life of Jesus), especially in the early existence of a people (the Christians), and embodying their ideas as to their origin, their gods, natural phenomena, etc." This myth was given classic form and prodigious condensation in the Gospel of John: "God so loved the world that he gave his only begotten son to the end that all that believe in him should not perish but have everlasting life."

Myths in this third category may be secular or religious. That is, they may issue in a religious faith or constitute part of the folklore of a people. But they give expression to proposed answers to ultimate questions, and represent a sincere quest for truth by those who initiate them. They may be proved inadequate or false by subsequent insights and knowledge. But, as long as they are viable for a people, they have a "given" quality and come to be accepted "on faith" as revelations. There is more in them of art than of science, though their credibility is always dependent on the growing scientific and changing philosophical ideas of a people. One could say a myth represents for those who embrace it the truth in the sphere with which it deals. Myths that are genuinely operative in the lives of individuals have the capacity to orient and to integrate all other thoughts and activities with reference to themselves, for they embody the conviction that the god or gods of whom they speak are jealous and demanding and that their will affects every aspect of a man's life.

We could of course seek to avoid misunderstanding by referring to the Christ "truth" or "image" or "metaphor" instead of the Christ "myth." All of these alternatives are applicable and relevant. But "myth" is the most inclusive and descriptive term. Myth is the best language religion has for communicating the peculiar insights it believes it possesses into ultimate truth. Therefore, when fresh insight or knowledge "makes ancient good uncouth" and forces the particular religion to demythologize, it can survive as a religion only if it successfully remythologizes.

Some myths may remain static indefinitely with some of their constituency, despite changing world-views in contemporary society that impinge upon them. They may indeed survive in substantially the same form for centuries, despite their incompatibility with other elements in contemporary world-views. But in this case they remain static, frozen, for those who continue to profess them. On the other hand, they may become extinct in the sense that they no longer live in the hearts of any body of believers.

The other possibility is that a given myth may evolve and be progressively remythologized as devout believers continue to proclaim the core of truth in the original myth which must now undergo adaptation and change if the new formulation of the myth, or "fabulous narrative," is to be compatible with new elements in man's evolving world-view. We are maintaining that the deepest and most authentic religious motivation is in any case to keep the world one, to find acceptable only that myth which enables everything else in man's knowledge, intuition, and experience to "hang together" in a convincing and compelling way.

Let us be entirely honest and openly make the judgment we are implying here. From the perspectives we are advocating, those religious beliefs which still proclaim a myth, or a form of a myth, which cannot be persuasively integrated with the contemporary world-view, embodying consensus on scientific and philosophical truth, are failing to live up to their responsibility toward modern man. At the same time, we must also frankly admit that individual adherents of the outmoded beliefs may well be morally and spiritually superior to other individuals who hold more viable beliefs.

This book does not presume to propose a new myth. New myths do not come into being by deliberate, rational process. But I do hope to articulate a new version of the ancient Christ myth which I believe is emerging as new truths of comparatively recent revelation demand that we demythologize in order to remythologize. We shall consider specifically what it is in these two new perspectives, evolution and depth psychology, that requires significant change in the formulation of the traditional myth. We shall undertake to demonstrate with selected illustrations from history that the evolving Christ myth has *always* had a life of its own.

Again, as we have said, myth is the only language religion can speak to express the truth on which it is founded. A myth is an idea, a metaphor, to reflect in outward and visible signs of written and spoken words an inward and spiritual grace. But the moment it is taken as literally true it may become a graven image, and professed belief in it may become an unrecognized form of idolatry. The greatest images and metaphors in poetry are those which seem to be working on several levels, whose depths are never fully plumbed. So in true religion. A myth must be kept fluid and flexible, not frozen and fixed, so that it can evolve as man's perception of religious truth evolves.

In this book I shall not be pleading for any finality in this proposed new version of the historical Christ myth. I shall be pleading, rather, for consideration of a remythologized form to help preserve in the milieu of a particular contemporary world-view the crucial kernel of truth in the original myth.

The Hebrew Angle of Vision

Clinical psychology demonstrates that what we see in any given instance depends upon the angle of our vision. If this angle is changed, or if physical elements in the field of vision—like lighting or coloring or distance—are changed, what we see may appear quite different. What we see is also dependent upon what the individual mind brings to the impression by way of memory and predisposition, what it may be expecting to see.

When Jesus of Nazareth raised the question, "But who

do you say that I am?" those around him made varying responses. Certain Pharisees saw him as a rival teacher whose message, if accepted, would give theirs the lie. They branded him heretic. Some of the chief priests who felt threatened in authority called him a blasphemer. Pilate and Herod saw him as a disturber of the peace which it was their responsibility to maintain. Many common people heard him gladly because he brought a message of hope that spoke to their condition. They recognized in him a man who "spoke as one having authority, and not as the scribes." Others, consumed with immediate problems and concerns of their own, turned a curious glance his way and quickly returned to their own preoccupations. Some sick and possessed persons were healed by him and proclaimed him magician, wonder-worker. Peter, after intimate companionship in the heat and burden of many days, responded: "Thou art the Christ, the son of the living God."

All of the disciples were Jews. This constituted in some sense the angle of their vision. They brought to their appraisal the contemporary expectation of a coming Messiah. As we shall presently recollect, already several versions of the Messiah myth were abroad in contemporary Judaism. Not only did these versions differ, they contained conflicting testimony. Jesus, as well as the disciples, must have brooded on the implications of the various prophecies. Inevitably they made their own value judgments concerning the kind of Messiah they would anticipate. Jesus carried the additional burden, in the quest of his own identity, of determining the relationship between the prophecies and his own mission. Ultimately the disciples and their converts in the early church confirmed Peter's initial assessment. They called Jesus "the Messiah," "the Christ," and saw in him the fulfillment of all the prophecies, sometimes oblivious to any inherent contradictions in the existing concepts. Moreover they were prepared to embrace new concepts concerning the attributes of "the Christ."

They were the inheritors of the Messiah myth, a fabulous narrative already in process of changing and evolving, which had sprung from the collective unconscious of the Jewish people in response to the traumatic experience of the loss of the united kingdom under David, subsequent division, successive military defeat and exile. First articulated by visionaries, of the substance dreams are made of, the various forms of the fabulous narrative could achieve the potency of a religious myth only through spontaneous confirmation by the collective unconscious of a substantial majority of the whole people.

In the shaping of a myth, first comes the compelling need, at least seven-eighths of which lies submerged beneath the level of consciousness. The Jews had known their greatest fulfillment, individually and corporately, under the reign of David the king. The nostalgia for the recovery of those golden days, no doubt immeasurably enhanced by the aesthetic distance of many generations, was as deeply motivated as the very drive to achieve and to retain identity, a drive which lies at the core of the mystery of human personality and community. Something in the unconscious of the Hebrew people told them with nagging persistence that they would never be themselves again until that kingdom was restored under a new David.

Since under David there had been a coincident achievement of nationhood and of a sense of solidarity as a religious community under God, religious and secular aspirations were fused into one infinite longing, powerful enough to give birth to the Messiah myth. The initial form which the myth took was that Yahweh would send a new David, a descendant of David, who would crush the enemies of Israel and restore the beloved kingdom. There were to be numerous refinements of the original myth as it began to evolve, including the Son of Man, the Suffering Servant, and the Logos versions. Moreover, in some variations of the Son of David version, the warlord was transformed into a Prince of Peace.

The Perspective of Contemporary Non-Jews

Jesus and his disciples were looking for a Messiah, whatever variations on the great theme they individually may have chosen. Their prescientific world-view presented no obstacles to their anticipation of the Messiah's coming in one or another or some combination of the forms prophesied. In presenting Jesus as the Christ to non-Jews, Paul and the author of the Fourth Gospel were constrained to become apologists for this initially Jewish faith, that is, to interpret it in ways which would make the new Messiah myth, the Christ myth, acceptable to non-Jews who brought to it a different world-view. These non-Jews were not looking for a Messiah in the Old Testament sense. When it came to the restoration of the Jewish nation they could not have cared less. But they were looking for a personal savior who could save them from enemies from without and within, and, bringing them as it were to themselves, could make possible for them a life more abundant, of which they sometimes dreamed but which they knew not how to attain.

They were even looking for a new God to worship, for they were living in the time of the death of their own Roman and Greek gods. Their adoration capacity was operating in a vacuum. The so-called mystery religions had sprung up and were competing for converts. The notion was rife that some form of rebirth into a more satisfying plane of being might be possible by mystical union, through some secret ritualistic practice, with a new and more efficacious god. Their angle of vision was that of various currents in the contemporary Greco-Roman culture. They brought to the Christ myth the philosophical and psychological presuppositions influenced by Platonic, Aristotelian, and Stoic thought, sometimes tinged with Gnosticism.

Throughout the apostolic and the early church periods, extending through the fifth century, there was continued reflection and debate on the evolving Christ myth. The Messiah myth, embodying the expectation of the advent of a saviour of the Jewish people, had evolved into a Christ myth proclaiming a universal saviour for all mankind, identified as Jesus of Nazareth.

As the Messiah myth had sprung from and found confirmation in the collective unconscious of the Jewish people under the dual compulsion of grief and a need to recover identity, so the emerging Christ myth assumed evolving shape as it moved from its Jewish inception to confirmation by the only partly conscious quest of non-Jews for a new God they could worship in spirit and in truth. We might say, in anticipation of more careful documentation later, that these were the proximate sources of the new myth and of its extraordinary vitality. It has been said that he who teaches me of my meanings is master of all I am. The new myth mastered men because, by virtue of the great apologists of the faith in the early church, it gave plausible answer to their ultimate questions. The fabulous narrative in its classic New Testament form,

God so loved the world that he gave his only begotten son to the end that all that believe in him should not perish but have everlasting life,

spoke to the condition, to the unconscious as well as the conscious needs of Jews and non-Jews alike. The current world-view in most of its variations permitted intellectual acceptance and affirmation of the new myth while it continued to raise questions that demanded refinement of the myth in the successive creeds.

The Ultimate Source of the Myth

Later we shall substantiate these proximate sources for the initiation and confirmation of the myth. Here for the moment we must further anticipate our argument by pointing to the fact that in addition to the proximate sources of the myth there was also an ultimate source, else the evolving Christ myth should not have found continuing confirmation in the human psyche down the ages amid changing world-views. The ultimate source of this myth is to be sought in the unconscious of men, all men, as we shall maintain. In response to the perennial questions on the conscious level, What would the perfect man be like? and What sort of community would he build? the unconscious of the Judo-Christian West has made reply in the form of archetypal images of "the Christ" and "the kingdom of God." These were given conscious expression through myth. Again, it is the unconscious, individually and corporately, that either confirms or rejects. And once more the conscious mind labors to give reasons.

What I am suggesting here is that the Messiah myth, from the beginning, had even deeper roots in the unconscious than the Jews' psychological need to recover identity. Powerful as that unconscious motivation was in projecting the apocalyptic dream of a new David, from our recently acquired perspective of depth psychology we can perceive in it also an achetypal image representing Judaism's early answer to the more universal question proposed by the conscious mind: What would the ideal man be like?

We shall presently see how that image evolves in its

various representations in the Old Testament and the Apocrypha. Had it not expanded to include Son of Man and Suffering Servant images by the time Jesus came along, no one, least of all Jesus himself, would have thought to identify him with it. The very titles Son of David and Son of Man suggest an unwitting movement from the particular to the universal. Israel's archetypal image of perfect manhood, still Jewish no doubt to the core, had assumed a new epithet, "Son of Man," marking a stage of evolution in the fabulous narrative that might begin to draw the attention of all men everywhere.

Archetypal images irresistibly require representation in some form. These images can reach across centuries and find confirmation in the unconscious of others. Does this account perhaps, from a depth-psychological perspective, for the creation of Michelangelo's "David"? Looking at Michelangelo's masterpiece, do we not see the archetypal image of perfect manhood, the Son of Man, as well as David the king or the Son of David? Is it not this shared archetypal image, alive in the collective unconscious, that elicits from us a confirmation beyond what our rational or cultivated aesthetic sense could provide? In the grace and power, the gentleness and majesty of that figure, do we not behold the warrior Son of David already transformed into the Son of Man, Prince of Peace?

The artist's conscious intention was clearly to portray the historic figure of David the shepherd, the psalmist, Jonathan's friend, Saul's compassionate therapist, Absalom's devoted father, rather than the brash youth boasting of his triumph over Goliath, the sly seducer of Naboth's wife, or the ruthless warlord reveling in military victory. But is not what our own unconscious perceives and responds to something infinitely more universal and archetypal? And is not this something given miraculous expression in a phrase in a psalm attributed to David which is otherwise, incongruously, a prayer of thanksgiving, exulting in military conquest: "Thy gentleness hath made me great"? The statue is saying it was David's gentleness that was his own ultimate claim to greatness. And in the "yea" that shouts from the depths of our own unconscious as we ponder this figure's deeper message do we not recognize an archetypal image whose essential witness is that man's major claim to greatness is the potential for gentleness that lives within him, and that, whatever else he may be like, the Son of Man *must* be like that?

I am leaping from the earliest Son of David Messiah image to the later Son of Man image to Michelangelo's image of David to the confirmation we experience in our own unconscious in order to demonstrate in one stroke the inherent capacity which that earliest Messiah myth contained for adaptation and viable evolution. While distinctively Jewish and even dated within Judaism, it carried within it a seed that could flower in other cultures and other ages because its roots lay in the collective unconscious of the species.

Myths Must Evolve to Survive

At this point I am asking for your tentative consent to the proposition that religious myths, fabulous narratives springing by inspiration from the mysterious depths of the unconscious of some mighty religious genius or geniuses, and gaining consent from the unconscious of countless other souls, do exhibit the capacity to evolve as a concomitant aspect of the evolving phenomenon of man. Later I hope to substantiate this claim with more convincing documentation, and, in Chapter V, to suggest ways in which the Christ myth is evolving today. For the present it is enough to agree that as man's angle of vision changes, what he sees changes, though what he is looking at may ultimately be revealed as one and the same.

The corollary to this proposition that myths may evolve is that if they are to remain viable in terms of capacity for integration within evolving world-views, they *must* evolve. Of course it is possible for versions of a particular myth to remain static for centuries and still hold in thrall large numbers of devotees, even as some species in biological evolution remain static within evolving ecological systems. We can witness this phenomenon today in religion as well as in contemporary flora and fauna. But one has the feeling that the main current of life has passed them by, whether religious sects or animal species. They carry within their very members the pathos of anachronism and stand under the judgment of possible extinction, the fate of some species both of religions and of animals that have lacked an adaptive capacity.

Ever since the Renaissance, individual Christians have demanded radical change in the articulation of the fabulous narrative. They have known that the Christ myth must not be permitted to remain crystallized forever by the Council of Chalcedon, that it must be allowed to continue to evolve if it is to retain credibility for modern man. The dawning age of science presaged the demand that deductive reasoning from historic revelation must be superseded even in religion by the inductive process. Happily there had always been in all the great religious traditions the apostolic succession of the mystics. This curious company, incidentally the only great religious tradition to insist on equality of the sexes from the beginning, had always characteristically but quite unwittingly practiced the inductive method afforded by first-hand religious experience and experimentation. We shall have occasion to consider their distinctive witness; for the Christian mystics, beginning with Paul, intuitively recognizing the distinction between symbol and reality, have always been more prepared than other men to accept change in the evolving myth.

Our Altered Angle of Vision

The world we see is no longer the same world seen by Jesus and the authors of the New Testament. The angle of our vision, without and within, has been changed and therefore our world-view is not the same. If there is conflict between our world-view and a cherished religious myth, that myth will either have to evolve to attain compatibility with it, or it will die for us; and this in the name of true religion which is constrained above all else "to get it all together." For the modern man we have defined, the only tenable world-view is one which has been shaped by the perspective of biological space-time, or duration. This is the new light that illumines all facts. This is the curve which all lines of thought must henceforth follow if they are to be accepted as thinkable and true. If the Christ myth is to be thinkable and true for this modern man, its lines must begin to follow this curve as it continues to evolve.

What is this new angle of vision, more specifically, and how does it affect what we see when we look at our world, at man, at Jesus of Nazareth, at the traditional Christ myth?

In the first place it is clearer than ever before that we do indeed dwell in a uni-verse, one in which everything is ultimately interdependent, everything interpenetrates everything else, and one set of laws operates throughout. The subjective experience of the mystic that it is one world in which everything interrelates and hangs together is increasingly being objectively confirmed by scientific investigation and discovery. The relatively new science of ecology is dramatically demonstrating just how pervasive the fact of interdependence really is.

The universe is itself the overarching and all-inclusive ecological system upon which all other ecological systems of smaller spatial areas are ultimately dependent. The universe is itself evolving. It may be expanding. It is certainly changing. As there continue to be new things under our sun, we can assume that there are new things under other suns in our universe. But despite the presence of change and innovation, there appear to be laws which operate within this universe and which remain the same yesterday, today and, as far as we can tell, forever. However random, fortuitous, "opportunistic" evolution may be, it nevertheless takes place within rules that are themselves invariable. Of all possible universes the imagination of man could conceive, we have this one and no other. Like Margaret Fuller, who was reported to Thomas Carlyle as having learned to accept the universe, and received the grudging recognition, "Gad, she'd better," we too had better learn to accept the universe we live in.

Contained within this vast, ecological, evolving system, the universe, is our world, the earth, this little planet that is our precarious craft hurtling through space and controlled in its own orbit by our sun. It is our best guess that our earth was born from a larger mass that included the sun through some kind of interstellar collision or near collision. Such collision may take place again, putting an end to the earth as we know it. We are also aware of the so-called second law of thermodynamics in which all matter in motion tends to slow down and to cool off. Given eons of time, life as we now know it on this planet may become impossible through either interstellar collision or the operation of this law.

Nevertheless, while this demonstrable law of thermodynamics describes an aspect of the universe as running down and cooling off, we now know a great deal about another aspect of the universe, at least on this planet, which can only be described as spiraling upward and warming up: *the evolution of life.* There is no sign within the process itself of any loss of vitality. Rather, as Teilhard de Chardin convincingly demonstrates, the movement is one from simple forms to ever more complex forms.

Teilhard describes this basic characteristic of evolution as increasing *complexification.* But it is a complexification in which an accompanying unification is preserved. This unification has two aspects: interior and exterior. The evolving plant or animal must retain, as it changes and grows, an interior integration and coordination if it is to survive. At the same time it must preserve a viable exterior unification in terms of ecological interpenetration with its environment. The total process, inward and outward, may be called adaptation. No plant or animal ever evolves by becoming simpler. Either it successfully adapts as it complexifies or it becomes extinct.

Teilhard makes use of another metaphor to point to another characteristic of the process. He speaks of the dimension of "within-ness" in all living things. This is the potential for growth and change that lies darkly hidden within. It is not merely that living things are altered by changes in external environment. It is that a given species carries within it a potential for development along certain lines. This potential cannot be described as infinite possibility. The species can evolve only within limitations, physical, mental, and psychological, prescribed by adaptations already made in its evolutionary past. Evolutionary advance, therefore, must be seen not only as an adaptation to changing exterior stimuli but as an unfolding or blossoming forth of a potential already present as a seed in the ancestry of the species.

In addition, one can think of what might be described as the sap of consciousness running up through the entire tree of life. Some researchers are even telling us of the possibility of very primitive forms of consciousness within plant life. In any case, with animal life one can describe the advance of evolution in terms of a spiraling upward of forms of consciousness. The highly evolved animal becomes more and more aware of more and more elements in its environment. The animal, man, has realized an incomparable breakthrough on the scale of evolution by achieving the faculty of reflection. His mobility, perceptiveness, mental capacity for concentration, study, and inductive analysis have made it possible for him to be increasingly aware of more and more aspects of his physical environment and their interrelatedness.

At the same time, his capacity to reflect has enabled him to cultivate a direct inward perception of moral and spiritual values which lie beyond the response and measuring faculties of the five traditional senses. In other words, he has only recently become aware of unseen elements in the universe which reside mysteriously within himself and other men as values which he has named: mercy, gentleness, tenderness, compassion, love. He extrapolates the theory that these must spring from some deeper source and have some transcendental support beyond the experience of their immediacy and immanence. But he knows that these convictions are ultimately conjectures and cannot be proved. One thing is clear: evolution has become conscious of itself in man. He is the first animal, so far as we can tell, to be aware it is evolving.

This leap of insight which has come to man as a result of the discovery of the fact of evolution is scarcely more than a century old. It has been assimilated as yet only by the consciousness of relatively few men, those we have chosen with Teilhard to call modern in this distinctive sense. But, at the same time, this insight may plausibly be claimed as perhaps the most important self-discovery man has ever made. From another point of view, as we have acknowledged, it is a revelation so profound and far-reaching that all other earlier revelations must be "trued up" to it, must in a certain sense be assimilated by it. They can remain thinkable and true only if they can coherently cohabit with this new revelation in one integrated world-view. In particular, to refer to one sphere, this revelation looms far above all the other revelations of modern science in its inherent importance for man's self-understanding and for the remythologizing he must engage in if his theology is to remain relevant.

The source and spring of evolution as well as its ultimate end, if we can even speak intelligently of a beginning and an end, are completely enshrouded in mystery. Nevertheless, man is able to place himself in space and time since the mysterious advent of life on this planet as has never been possible for him before. It would be impossible to overestimate the magnitude of this revelation in its implications with reference to our inherited theological doctrines or metaphors, especially the traditional Christ myth.

Enthusiasm Tamed by Metaphor

In the first blush of man's response to this extraordinary fact about his past and its inherent implications for his future, some were carried away with humanistic enthusiasm for the future of the species. They could see only an *élan vital* which, because it had been preserved so successfully in man's antecedents against such incredible odds, must surely move onward and spiral upward forever. This natural and pardonable optimism gave rise to the excesses of the liberal movement within theology. For many the rude awakening came with the first and second world wars. Disillusionment has been further substantiated by the phenomena on a worldwide scale of pollution, overpopulation, profligate wastage of the earth's nonreplacable resources of energy, and the development of nuclear weapons whose extensive use could put an untimely end to life as we know it on this planet.

Teilhard's invincible optimism persisted in his conviction of the gradual "Christification" of the universe as the Point Omega of the entire process. As I shall develop later, I too entertain the hope of a gradual Christification of man as he continues to evolve. I see "onward and upward" as a precarious opportunity that is offered man in the foreseeable future, which is after all only a limited distance ahead. Our vision cannot penetrate very far into the future, measured on the scale of evolution. Had there been a sentient being on the face of the earth while man's forebears yet lived in the trees, could he have foreseen the advent of man?

Even on a clear day no one can see forever, despite the irresistible appeal of the popular song. On a day when the mind is cleared of the fog of despair and depression, it *can* see the possibility of better days ahead for mankind if certain objectives can be achieved: abandonment of national arms as anachronistic in "one world", a progressive purification of the environment, conservation and sharing of the existing sources of energy and the harnessing of new ones, wider voluntary birth control. But on the scale of observation of evolution, while we can see very far backward in time, we can see only a comparatively few moments ahead, even with regard to necessary change if man is to survive.

Within the context of the all-embracing fact of evolution, how can we any longer conceive an eschatological end of the times? When the inherent characteristics of the process are endless movement and change, how can we think of a time when the universe shall have arrived? So while I personally owe so much to Teilhard in the articulation of my own vision and hope, I must early confess that I have quarrels with him at some crucial points. I find it impossible to foresee *any* end to the process of evolution, much less an *inevitable* Christification of the universe. Robert Frost once said that the only enthusiasm he could accept was one that had been "tamed by metaphor." In the present context, my enthusiasm for man's future has been tamed by the inescapable and ever threatening metaphor which the fact of evolution has itself provided: possible extinction.

Extinction of a species has always come about through some form of overspecialization which blocked effective adaptation. When one ponders the areas in which man is currently overspecializing—use of technology for the manufacture of destructive weapons while virulent nationalization is rampant, emphasis on prolonging life without compensating birth control, extravagant consumption of vital materials producing simultaneous shortage and lethal pollution of the environment—one realizes the terrible risks we are running. Bertrand Russell once observed that it would be a pity if man should cease to exist because he seems to have something of value left in him. One is reminded also of the story of the man who said to his executioner in the French Revolution as the guillotine was about to fall on his head: "It seems a pity to cut it off; I think it still has something in it." We can smile, but the pathos inherent in the real possibility of the extinction of the species runs very deep. Harlow Shapley has said there are perhaps a million planets in the known cosmos capable of supporting life. But that there are actually any forms of life elsewhere which constitute or could evolve into sentient beings is something we do not and perhaps cannot know. If the only sentient being on this planet goes, where else would one look for his like?

Teilhard himself, at an earlier period, experienced the peculiar *angst* of modern man. He referred to this malady as the "sickness of the dead-end—the anguish of feeling shut in, of not being sure, and of not seeing how [one] ever could be sure, that there is an outcome, a suitable outcome, to that evolution."

Teilhard's Ultimate Faith

This is a terror of greater magnitude than even that experienced by Pascal as he gazed at the immensity of the heavens. The dimensions of Teilhard's vision had been expanded beyond measure. But by pursuing the scientific quest he came at length upon the "complement and necessary corrective to this malady," which he describes as "the perception of an evolution animating these dimensions."

Indeed time and space become humanized as soon as a definite movement appears which gives them a physiognomy. We have only to think and to walk in the direction in which the lines passed by evolution take on their maximum coherence.[5]

Meantime, Teilhard's intellectual quest for meaning and design in the evolutionary process was undergirded by a recurring mystical experience which was crucial to the realization of the ultimate synthesis at which he arrived. With characteristic modesty he shares it with us in a footnote in *The Divine Milieu:*

Throughout my life, by means of my life, the world has little by little caught fire in my sight until, aflame all around me, it has become almost completely luminous from within. Such has been my experience in contact with the earth—the diaphany of the Divine at the heart of the universe on fire; Christ, his heart, a fire, capable of penetrating everywhere and gradually spreading everywhere.[6]

[5] Teilhard de Chardin, *The Phenomenon of Man*, p. 233.
[6] Teilhard de Chardin, *The Divine Milieu* (New York: Harper & Row, 1965), p. 46.

At the same time, though the diaphany of the Divine which he perceived at the heart of matter was the Christ, so deeply did he come to trust the world itself that he believed he would retain his faith in it even should his quest of truth compel him to forgo his traditional Christian faith.

If as a result of some interior revolution, I were successfully to lose my faith in Christ, my faith in a personal God, my faith in the Spirit, I think that I would still continue to believe in the world. The world (the value, the infallibility, the goodness of the world). That in the last analysis is the first and last thing in which I believe. It is by this faith that I live, and it is to this faith, I feel, that at the moment of death, mastering all doubts, I shall surrender myself. I surrender myself to this undefined faith in a single and infallible World, wherever it may lead me.[7]

How can anything shake such a faith as this? Dostoevski once said that if he were compelled to choose between truth and Christ he would unhesitatingly choose Christ. I think Teilhard is saying that, if he were constrained to make this choice as a result of his devotion to scientific inquiry, he would choose truth because his ultimate faith was "in a single and infallible world." In the end he was able "to get it all together," preserving his Christian faith as well, enormously expanded in what must be the most extraordinary synthesis since Thomas Aquinas.

I once asked a Jesuit priest if he did not think this the case. He made an interesting reply: "Perhaps it would be more accurate to say that he will play Abelard to some new Aquinas. I accept this possibility—that the poet-seer in him exceeded his capacity to compose a new systematic theology. We must all attempt to carry forward this unfinished work. Meantime I continue to resonate to this invincible faith in the world, especially in the process of

7 Henri de Lubac, *Teilhard de Chardin, the Man and His Meaning* (New York: Mentor-Omega Book, New American Library, 1967), p. 132.

evolution in which we perceive and can celebrate as "very good," continuing creation.

The New Direction for the Evolving Christ Myth

Now what demands does this new evolutionary perspective place upon our contemporary Christology? How shall its lines begin to follow this curve? In the first place, we must see the world as dynamic rather than static. We can no longer speak of eternal essences. Human nature is itself in process of changing. If there were a heaven and a hell they too would be evolving in the nature of the universe that has so recently been revealed to us. Instead of a finished creation which God beheld and called "very good" but later looked at again, and, finding very bad in man, was constrained to readjust by the intervention of his only Son, we now perceive a continuing creation in which man is one of the most recent products. He is still in process of being "hominized" to use another of Teilhard's coined words.

It is not necessary to remake man by putting aside the laws already set in motion. The incarnation in Jesus cannot be seen any longer as a new creation, amending the first creation; it must be perceived as a new event in continuing creation. The incarnation has been present in the "within-ness" of the process all the way up to the Christ event, including the countless aeons of time in this evolving universe before some molecular substance had become cellular substance. "The whole creation travaileth and groaneth together until now," as Paul recognized even without any knowledge of evolution. But this travailing and groaning within evolution must also be conceived as continuing creation.

There is no need for a miraculous birth. The greater miracle is that the seed that flowered in Jesus was present throughout the uncounted millennia of the process itself. Jesus is the first fully hominized man. He is the second Adam, the new man. In him a higher consciousness has broken through. He has burst the egg of evolution. Man, the first animal to be aware of the process of evolution, is therefore the first animal called to be a co-creator in the sense that he may choose, within the limitations that have been established in his nature, the future course of his own continuing evolution. Jesus is the "sport" (to use the technical term), the emergent, the pace-setting and path-finding mutation. In the new level of consciousness which he has attained, mankind may see the outlines of a new life-style, the kingdom style. Jesus said we won't know who he is unless the Holy Spirit in us reveals it to us. Interpreted in the present context, that is to say: "You won't want to follow in the way I have chosen unless something in the depths of your being resonates with a 'yea!' "

This new man we see in Jesus is *the Christ*, the Godlike man. This Christ is indeed God in human form, the only God we are capable of worshiping and adoring and aspiring to obey. Our conception of the Christ, as far as we are capable of looking into the future, will have to come under the plumbline of the Christ we have beheld and continue to behold in the Jesus of history through our reflection on the New Testament. But this Christ who is God in human guise is no longer to be thought of as co-extensive with the Jesus of history. He can be known in the depths of our own being, and we may catch glimpses of him in one another. This Christ within is not the Jesus of history but is the same Christ we have known first and foremost in him.

Here is another point of divergence between the thought of Teilhard, as I understand it, and my own. As far as I can see, he would identify Christ and Jesus in the traditional way. I believe we must begin to distinguish be-

tween Jesus and the Christ. To help us keep this distinction clear, I believe we should refrain from using the word
"Christ" as Jesus' surname, or as a prefix to his name, or
using interchangeably Christ and Jesus to designate the
historical man. We shall, on the other hand, be justified in
referring to "Jesus called the Christ," as Tillich and some
others have done with careful discrimination.

I believe that this is essential to a remythologizing of
the Christ myth in such a way as to make it viable in the
context of our evolving world-view. I believe we must
distinguish between Jesus and the Christ in order to
hold onto both: remain disciples of Jesus and passionate
believers in a Christ myth for our time. The necessary
details of revision of the metaphors of preexistence, incarnation, the two natures, atonement, resurrection, and
second coming within the traditional myth we shall consider in Chapter V. For the present it is necessary only to
have sketched the need for a remythologized Christ myth
to conform with our newly acquired perspectives of evolution and depth psychology.

II

The messiah myth of the old testament and the jesus of history

If we are successfully to remythologize the Christ myth so that it may become viable for modern man, we must begin by recollecting the Messiah myth as it presented itself in several versions to the young Jesus. We must project ourselves into his world in order that we may, at least in a measure, see from his angle of vision.

The children of Israel, remember, had developed their faith in their God concurrently with their realization of identity as a peculiar people, one nation with a king anointed by God himself. And while this united kingdom did not endure for long, the memory of what had been a peak of self-fulfillment lived on in the ineradicable nostalgia of the children of Israel, even when the kingdom broke in two and many were forced into exile. Something so traumatic as the dissolution of this theocracy threatened at once both their culture and their religion, and occasioned the greatest anxiety any person or community may experience: the fear of permanent loss of identity. So great was the compulsion to dream of the restoration of a new kingdom with a new king! Behind it was all the push of the generated fear of nonbeing, before it all the pull of "the courage to be."

The Psychological Source of the Messiah Myth

When the human psyche is confronted with an over-whelming need, for which there seems to be no likelihood of fulfillment in the normal course of events, the unconscious evokes fantasy to create a vision of an imagined fulfillment. As long as the current world-view permits a plausible distinction between the natural and the super-natural, a divine intervention may be conceived which is capable of accomplishing what no earthly power can be marshaled to effect. The Messiah myth recorded in the Old Testament was given birth by fantasy in just this way when the children of Israel were *in extremis*. One might say that the idea of a Messiah capable of putting this lost world together again sprang as an archetypal image from the collective unconscious of the children of Israel. This is not to say it was not also conceived by the Holy Spirit. And the prevailing world-view made it possible to adopt the dream as a plausible article of faith. Israel began to believe in a Messiah sent from on high who would destroy her enemies and reestablish the kingdom on earth.

The reigning king, in the days of the theocracy, had come to be regarded as the servant or minister of Yahweh. The process of anointing was instituted to symbolize this important concept. The Lord himself chose David among the sons of Jesse and personally instructed Samuel: "Rise and anoint him; this is the man" (1 SAMUEL 16:12). We are at once informed, "Then the spirit of the Lord came upon David and was with him from that day onwards" (1 SAMUEL 16:13).

"Messiah" means, literally, "the anointed one." We can see, therefore, the more immediate source of the Messiah myth in the place which the king held in the religious consciousness of the people by the time of David. As the historic king stood in relation to Yahweh, so would the eschatological king who was to come in order to restore the earthly kingdom. Even in its most advanced stages of development, the Messiah myth never equated "the anointed one" with the One who anoints. He is to be endowed with the spirit of Yahweh, but he is never confused with Yahweh.

Throughout the Old Testament, we can see how the prophesied Messiah (the King that was to come) would be able to be identified as the Jesus of history: the lineage of Jesus traced backward to David, the son relationship to a father God, and the universal and everlasting reign of the Son.

The Expanding Images of the Son of David

There are still other strands, springing from the pious imagination of the prophets as they brood over the future of Israel, that are later to find their way into the evolving Christ myth. During the impending disaster of the Assyrian invasion, Micah could dream: "But you, Bethlehem in Ephrathah, small as you are to be among Judah's clans, out of you shall come forth a governor for Israel, one whose roots are far back in the past, in days gone by" (MICAH 5:2). Apparently the archetypal image for which Israel is to look is now expanded to reach beyond David far back toward the origin of the race itself, perchance even to Adam in the Garden of Eden. One may well expect of such a figure a marvelous birth, and that he might be nourished with the food assigned the first king in paradise: "Therefore the Lord himself shall give you a sign: A young woman is with child, and she will bear a son, and will call him Immanuel. By the time that he has learnt to reject evil and choose good, he will be eating curds and honey" (ISAIAH 7:14–15). Even so, in the making of a myth, do images arising out of the unconscious relate at once to ideas concerning the origin of man, and to ideas concerning his future.

As the idea of the messianic figure develops, it characteristically becomes more universal in its application, and
there is a refinement of the Messiah's personality. Though
his mission will still include crushing the enemies of Israel, his spirit will be marked by magnanimity and he will
be known as the Prince of Peace. "Prince" probably because Yahweh, being a jealous God, will reserve the role
of King for himself: "For a boy has been born for us, a son
given to us to bear the symbol of dominion on his shoul-
der, and he shall be called in purpose wonderful, in battle
God-like, Father for all time, Prince of peace" (ISAIAH
9:6). Because the spirit of Yahweh, the real king, will be
fully reflected in the Prince, and because Yahweh's reign
is universal, even the animal kingdom will become peace-
able:

> Thus the wolf shall live with the sheep, and the
>   leopard lie down with the kid;
> The calf and the young lion shall grow up together
>   and a little child shall lead them;
> The cow and the bear shall be friends, and their
>   young shall lie down together.
> The lion shall eat straw like cattle;
> The infant shall play over the hole of the cobra,
>   and the young child dance over the viper's nest.
> They shall not hurt nor destroy in all my holy
>   mountains;
> For as the waters fill the sea,
> so shall the land be filled with the knowledge of the Lord.
>   ISAIAH 11:6-9

The Suffering Servant Image

It is not to be assumed that the process by which the
myth evolved contained only one strand and moved in

only one direction. With ideas, as with animals, it is a
matter of the survival of the fittest, or of the one that fits
the changing environment. And even with those most
viable strands that were destined to survive, interact with
the self-understanding of Jesus, and evolve into the Christ
myth, there were ups and downs, the purging of old associations and the assimilation of new ones.

We have referred to the movement toward universaliza-
tion, and the addition of the qualities of righteousness and
peacemaking. The author of chapters forty to fifty-five in
the book of Isaiah, referred to as Deutero-Isaiah or Second Isaiah, introduced a new idea which most scholars
agree was not originally messianic. In his prophecy of
things to come, the old notion of a Davidic king, still very
much alive in other contemporary strands and destined to
remain so even until the present in orthodox Judaism, is
abandoned. Instead, his vision presents, as an agent in the
fulfillment of Yahweh's purposes, the image of a Suffering
Servant. The process by which the new Israel will be ultimately victorious is one not of military conquest but of
redemptive suffering. In some passages this Servant is
described as if he were an individual:

> Behold my servant shall prosper,
> he shall be lifted up, exalted to the heights.
>   ISAIAH 52:13

Therefore I will allot him a portion with the great,
and he shall share the spoil with the mighty,
because he exposed himself to face death and was reckoned
    among transgressors,
because he bore the sin of many and interceded for their
    transgressions.
                                    ISAIAH 53:12

In other passages the Servant seems to be a metaphor for
the nation, Israel: "You are my servant, Israel, through

whom I shall win glory" (ISAIAH 49:3). Not until New
Testament times was this image of the Suffering Servant
identified with the Messiah. As we shall see presently,
perhaps Jesus himself was in part responsible for this
crucial turn taken by the one strand of the evolving myth.

At the same time, some of the strands where the figure
of the Messiah as king is retained, something of the idea of
redemptive suffering rather than military prowess creeps
in:

> Rejoice greatly, O daughter of Zion!
>   Shout aloud, O daughter of Jerusalem!
> Lo, your king comes to you,
>   triumphant and victorious is he,
> humble and riding on an ass,
>   on a colt the foal of an ass.
>
>   ZECHARIAH 9:9–10

The Son of Man Image

In Daniel there is the very important emergence of a
new symbol. Yahweh will send "one like a Son of man."
Again, though this figure is in retrospect identified as the
Messiah, the original idea represented something of a discontinuity, or at least an emergent or mutation in the
myth:

I was still watching in visions of the night and I saw one like
a [Son of] man coming with the clouds of heaven; he ap-
proached the Ancient in Years and was presented to him. Sovereignty and glory and kingly power were given to him, so that
all people and nations of every language should serve him; his
sovereignty was to be an everlasting sovereignty which should
not pass away, and his kingly power such as should never be
impaired.

                                    DANIEL 7:13–14

It is very important to recognize that this vision came in a dreamlike state, thus confirming the conviction of Carl Jung that the unconscious is the source of all first-hand religious experience. This archetypal image of the Son of Man has obvious affinities with the perfection of the first man, Adam, and lends itself, under the aspect of our new evolutionary perspective, to identification with this image of the new man, the "son of man" (i.e., man's successor) as well. Later, Jesus, in his quest of identity, will reflect upon this image for the understanding of his own mission, perhaps as a "forerunner."

Reconciliation of the Two Strands

Inevitably, much speculation arose as to the time of the arrival of the Messiah as well as to the exact nature of his work. Some rabbis felt that the impending dénouement would be signaled by a devastating increase of disasters: war, pestilence, famine, and chaos. Others felt that the time might be hastened by the penitence and obedience of the faithful. Still others foresaw the arrival presaged by a forerunner, variously designated as a return of Elijah, Moses, or Enoch, harking back to the prophecy of Malachi: "Look, I will send you the prophet Elijah before the great and terrible day of the Lord comes" (MALACHI 4:5).

In an attempt to reconcile the two divergent traditions, the mundane naturalistic king and the otherworldly, universal Son of Man, a new timetable was proposed: the messianic kingdom would succeed the present aeon and continue variously from forty to two thousand years, the millennium, to be followed by a new aeon, the final universal and timeless reign. II Esdras reflects the promise of the aeon beyond the millennium:

My son the Messiah shall appear with his companions and bring four hundred years of happiness to all who survive. At the end of that time, my son the Messiah shall die, and so shall all mankind who draw breath. Then the world shall return to its original silence for seven days as at the beginning of creation, and no one should be left alive. After seven days the age which is not yet awake shall be roused and the age which is corruptible shall die. The earth shall give up those who sleep in it, and the dust those who rest there in silence; and the storehouses shall give back the souls entrusted to them. Then the Most High shall be seen on the judgment seat, and there shall be an end of all pity and patience. Judgment alone shall remain, truth shall stand firm and faithfulness be strong; requital shall at once begin and open payment be made; good deeds shall awake and wicked deeds allowed to sleep.

II ESDRAS 7:28–35

In any event, by the time Jesus reached young manhood, all the strands of the evolving Messiah myth, from which the Christ myth was to take its earliest forms, lay at hand.

The Quest of the Historical Jesus

It seems reasonable to assume that the Apostolic Church would never have arrived at the conviction that Jesus was the Messiah, had not those still present, who knew him in the flesh, been able to reconcile this conclusion with what they had heard him say and seen him do. Much later, perhaps, the identification of the historical figure with the Messiah myth might have taken place without such corroboration, but it is inconceivable that those who were able to correct false projections by reason of personal recollection could have called Jesus Messiah unless they were persuaded that the title could plausibly be applied to the man they knew.

As Reginald H. Fuller has put it in *The New Testament in Current Study*, "We must at least try to show that the

THE MESSIAH MYTH AND JESUS

history of Jesus can bear the weight of its post-Easter interpretation in the kerygma (the kernel of the faith in the New Testament). . . . We have a right to demand that there should be a continuous frame of reference between Jesus and the kerygma."[1]

I am assuming that Jesus was fully man, that he enjoyed a natural birth from the union of a man and a woman, that he was subject to the human condition as are other men, but that in some extraordinary way faculties present in other men were in him enhanced to such a degree that he constituted among men a mutation, a "sport," a breakthrough from the evolutionary perspective. I am referring to his moral stature as a man, his compassion for, and mystical identification with, other men in their suffering and sorrow and especially in the tragic bondage in which their sin placed them, and his ability to interpret and to demonstrate a wholly new lifestyle which might be described as living presently and consciously in the kingdom.

He did "bestride the narrow world like some Colossus," not in terms of vaunted earthly power, but in terms of an inner confidence that he *knew*, as no one else before him, what God required of men, and that if men would but listen and follow he could show them how to abandon the old life of sin and embark here and now upon a new and fulfilled life. He spoke as no other man had spoken, in both manner and content. He spoke *as one having authority*.

What, then, did Jesus understand to be the source of this authority? Did he think of himself as rabbi, teacher, prophet, wonder-worker, or did he believe that he was called to some more exalted role? If so, how did he reach this conclusion?

We recognize that it is extremely difficult to determine

---

[1] Reginald H. Fuller, *The New Testament in Current Study* (New York: Charles Scribner's Sons, 1962), pp. 30–31.

what the authentic words of Jesus are and what constitute authentic reflections, through the authors of the Gospels, of Jesus' own self-understanding. The rise of the highly disciplined historical and linguistic studies known as Form Criticism which seek to identify the successive strata in the development of the New Testament has been a great help to us in determining what qualify as *logia*, that is, the authentic words of Jesus. But there remain many problems and unanswered questions.

There are no extant writings of Jesus' own, indeed no suggestion that any ever existed, save that he once wrote something in the sand, perhaps of no significance at all, to spare another unnecessary embarrassment. The authors of the New Testament and of other writings which may have constituted some of their sources were themselves not historians but theologians, however amateur by current standards. The authors of the four Gospels did not intend to write biographies under the discipline of historical accuracy in the modern sense, but were, rather, constrained to present treatises proclaiming the coming of the Messiah and supporting the claim by reference to the teaching, the deeds, and the person of one Jesus of Nazareth.

Highlights of the Quest in Recent Times

Beginning in the late eighteenth century and continuing through the nineteenth, there was a succession of scholars, largely German, who undertook to discover the authentic Jesus of history. Albert Schweitzer assigned himself the monumental task of recording the history of this effort, together with his own conclusions, in the masterpiece he called *The Quest of the Historical Jesus*. The last paragraph, appearing to despair of recovering the historical figure, turned to the Christ of faith:

He comes to us as One unknown, without a name, as of old, by the lake-side He came to those men who knew Him not. He speaks to us the same word: "Follow Thou me" and sets us to the tasks which He has to fulfill for our time. He commands. And to those who obey Him, whether they be wise or simple, He will reveal Himself in the toils, the conflicts, the sufferings which they shall pass through in His fellowship, and as an ineffable mystery, they shall learn in their own experience who He is.[2]

Despite the very narrow way by which we must come to the historical figure, I am persuaded that it is the only way that can lead into life for the modern man. There has been a tendency since Schweitzer to abandon the quest altogether on the ground that we can never hope to know the historical Jesus. It may be that we shall have to concede with R. H. Lightfoot: "For all the inestimable value of the gospels, they yield us little more than a whisper of His voice; we trace in them but the outskirts of His ways."[3]

Yet, precisely because Jesus was a man who once lived and walked upon this earth and was one about whom such tremendous claims were plausibly made, it is of supreme importance that we try to catch even this whisper of his voice and to trace in the Gospels "the outskirts of His ways." Granted the task is an extremely difficult one, indeed all but impossible, it must not be abandoned because we have reached a stage in man's development when, for the modern mind, it is the historical figure who must validate any form of the Christ myth we can continue to associate with him.

There has always been a conflict between the historian

---

[2] Albert Schweitzer, *The Quest of the Historical Jesus* (London: A. & C. Black, 1936), p. 401.

[3] R. H. Lightfoot, *History and Interpretation in the Gospels* (London and New York: Harper & Bros., 1935), p. 225.

and the theologian. Henry Cadbury, whose first loyalty is as a historian, has put it this way:

The historians and the theologians have a different sense of values. The latter think their sphere, the dramatic portrayal of human experience, is more relevant. They regard history as useless. They quite correctly gauge the difficulty of recovering Jesus. . . . They can claim that the Jesus of history has never been central in Christianity.[4]

So Rudolf Bultmann, who has perhaps had wider influence than any other contemporary New Testament scholar, wants to demythologize the cosmological elements in the New Testament, and even, apparently, the mythological claims about the death and resurrection of Jesus, and yet at the same time refuses to demythologize the central claim of the kerygma itself. The kerygma, he believes, is impregnable as the record of the existential experience of faith in response to the preached Christ.

Jesus Christ confronts men nowhere other than in the kerygma, as he had so confronted Paul and brought him to decision. The kerygma does not mediate historical knowledge [of Jesus] and one may not seek to get beyond the kerygma and use it to reconstruct the historical Jesus. Not the historical Jesus, but Jesus Christ, the preached Christ, is the Lord.[5]

Having said that "we can, strictly speaking, know nothing of the personality of Jesus,"[6] Bultmann concedes that the actual historicity of Jesus does, nevertheless, make all the difference:

The event of Christ is of a wholly different order from the cult myths of Greek or Hellenistic religion. Jesus Christ is certainly presented as the Son of God, a pre-existent divine being, and

---

[4] Henry Cadbury, *The Eclipse of the Historical Jesus* (Pendle Hill, Pa.: Pamphlet #133), p. 27.

[5] Quoted in *The Eclipse of the Historical Jesus*, p. 28.

[6] R. Bultmann, *Jesus and the Word* (New York: Harper Torchbooks, 1961), p. 9.

therefore to that extent a mythical figure. But he is also a con-
crete figure of history—Jesus of Nazareth. His life is more than
a mythical event; it is a human life which ended in the tragedy
of crucifixion.[7]

Happily, some of the post-Bultmannians like James M.
Robinson and Günther Bornkamm have embarked upon a
new quest of the historical Jesus, knowing that the alter-
native for the modern mind would be to lose interest in
any Christ myth which related to the Jesus of history.

Jesus' Childhood and Adolescence

We return to the central question, therefore. What can
we know, or at least assume with reasonable assurance,
about this Jesus?

First of all, it stands to reason that in his childhood the
historical Jesus was exposed to the stories, the poetry, the
myths that were presently to find their way into the canon
of the Old Testament. Alone among men the Hebrews had
accumulated, and preserved by cherishing them, the traditions, insights, and aspirations that could nourish the
childhood of one whom men would one day call the Son
of God. The very existence of these histories, prophecies,
songs of praise, and the reverence in which they were
held by those who imparted them to their children, constituted "the fulness of time" from which a prophet could
arise about whose person a new religion could plausibly
be created.

We may safely assume that, whatever other historical
justification there may have been for the ultimate exaltation of the mother of Jesus to the place of a fourth person
in a quaternity, inclusive of the hallowed Trinity, Mary

---

[7] R. Bultmann, *Kerygma and Myth* (New York: Harper Torchbooks,
1961), I: 34.

conveyed to the absorptive mind and spirit of this sensitive child all the reverence and wonder appropriate for a devout Jew with reference to this inheritance. And the human father, Joseph, whatever his strengths or his weaknesses, must have related to this child in such a way that the word "father" accumulated no negative freight in the unconscious, thus permitting Jesus one day to use this word with reference to God as if it were the most natural term available. Given the kind of filial relation Jesus felt and expressed toward God, in Freudian context the indirect testimony to the quality of Jesus' relationship to his earthly father is very impressive.

Did Mary and Joseph entertain the hope for their first born that he might one day qualify as Messiah? We cannot know. At least it would have been psychologically possible, if not probable, that devout Jews like themselves should long for a son who would stand in the great succession of Hebrew prophets. Certainly it is a sound assumption that the characteristic of supreme self-confidence as an interpreter of the kingdom which Jesus was later to exhibit in word and manner must have had its source far back in early childhood. Psychologically we know that a ripened self-confidence and self-love in maturity have their antecedents in the confirming love and expectations of those who minister to the child in the formative years.

The first story about the growing child, his appearance in the temple at twelve, confidently expounding Scripture to mature, professional scholars and priests, may not be historically accurate in detail, but is very likely poetically true because psychologically sound. The near arrogance of the later self-assurance ("It has been said by them of old time, but *I* say unto you") must have had its dramatic antecedents in childhood.

We have not a single portrait of Jesus in adolescence— the period in which the major battles are fought in that

interior arena where identity is won from the whole ter-
rifying range of what to every callow youth must seem
"infinite possibility." What roles did Jesus play in imagination during periods of poignant solitude in his youth?
What were the figures and images in the Old Testament
with which he identified? The fertility of his imagination,
the poetic and dramatic quality of the images which en-
livened this imagination, are later to be reflected in the
parables which his artistic genius shaped to convey the
truths he passionately experienced. We can assume that as
an adolescent he brooded endlessly upon the questions:
Who am I? What do I want to be and to do?

Moreover, these universal questions, inescapable for the
sensitive and intelligent young person, are always given
answer finally through the mysterious dialectical process
of interaction between the ego's inner quest and the
changing realities of actual relationship. We do not know
that any of those who were friends or disciples in his
mature years were friends or acquaintances of his youth.
But there is no evidence that unusual seclusion characterized this period. He must then have known other young
men and women when he was what we would now call a
teenager.

How did they see him and how did he see them? Surely
he could not have arrived later at the intuitive wisdom
reflected by the insight of the author of the Fourth Gospel, "for he knew what was in man," unless at this early
period he had come into vital and intimate relationship
with his peers. One comes to know himself largely by
interaction with others who are discovering who they are,
exploring together the boundaries both of identification
and counter-distinction. Who were those he especially
loved among his peers, both male and female, and why?
Who were those who put him off and why? We cannot
know the answers, but it is of great importance to recognize the legitimacy of the questions.

The Mature Years

One has the impression that by the time he assumed his ministry he had decided, for whatever reason, to forgo marriage. Was it the imminence of the impending kingdom that made sexual gratification and the rearing of children irrelevant? Did he embrace the single life vocationally, choosing to be unencumbered by the responsibility of marriage in order to move more freely and to dedicate his time and energies more fully to the proclamation of the kingdom?

The psychodynamics of the man-woman relationship are operative in all personal, vital contact between the sexes, whether there is overt sexuality or not. Kazantzakis's imaginative treatment of a conjectural "last temptation" is psychologically sound. The juxtaposition of conflicting emotions, and the resultant ironies, presented in the rock opera *Jesus Christ Superstar*, ring a bell as an inevitable part of what must have been the true life story of Jesus that never found its way into the Gospel. Mary Magdalen's perplexity, "I don't know how to love him" and her poignant "I love him so, he scares me so" must have been a part of the inwardness of the experience of the women he drew to him. Mary's combination of emotions in this musical piece, containing elements of woman-lover and mother-protector, are inescapable aspects of what must have constituted the complexity of the man-woman encounter with Jesus. The haunting lines imputed to this Mary at any rate strike a responsive chord in the heart of the listener and make the historical figure suddenly more relevant and strangely contemporary.

The very fact that in the New Testament there is so little jealousy and the kind of tension created by the usual possessiveness of the man-woman relationship is itself evidence that during the brief span of his public ministry,

one to three years, Jesus deliberately refrained from close
relationship with any one woman.

What about relationship with individual men? If the
author of the Fourth Gospel is indeed the apostle John, or
one interpreting his message for him, what is the inwardness of the emotions behind the veiled expression, "the
beloved disciple" with reference to himself? Is there reflected in this enigmatic phrase a personal relationship of
greater depth than the other male disciples were privileged to experience? Certainly there is at least an awareness on the part of this disciple of a very special, life-
giving feeling of personal confirmation by Jesus which
had been transforming to him. He and his brother, James,
had called upon the Master to rain down fire from heaven
upon the inhospitable Samaritans. In one Gospel, they are
reported to have requested favored places for themselves
at the anticipated banquet in the kingdom; in another,
their mother makes the demand. Yet, if the author is John,
he appears to have mastered his violent temper and abandoned overweening ambition in favor of the humility
becoming a servant who has been called a friend.

But what did Jesus do with the tumultuous emotions
that invade the consciousness of all young men and
women almost in proportion as they are vital persons?
Are we to assume some placid sexlessness, devoid of passion? What we see in the fully developed man is passion
transmuted into compassion. What he is reported to have
said is that he who looks upon a woman to lust after her
has already committed adultery with her in his heart. In
the first place, this carnal desire isn't really the same as
the overt act of adultery, since no one's person is actually
violated. In the second place, the judgment is patently too
harsh and smacks of "holier than thou" if it springs from
one who was by his own standard without sin. Did Jesus
never look upon a woman with inward desire for her? To

maintain that he did not is to call into question the gen-
uineness of his manhood. Many of us should instinctively
respect him less, not more, if it could be proved conclu-
sively that Jesus never desired a woman. The relevance and
applicability of his message to our lives in this important
area of human experience would be diminished, not
heightened, as the Church has sometimes assumed.

We know that emotions of anger welled up in the Jesus
of history. The stinging recriminations against the enemies of his message, "hypocrites," "whited sepulchres,"
can scarcely have been falsely imputed to him. They ring
true. Did he then never experience sexual desire? There is
no evidence that he did. But does any virile man escape
this human passion? If one truly believes in his full humanity, and given the passionate, zestful characteristics
depicted in other contexts in the New Testament, one is
driven to believe that Jesus too must have been guilty of
the sin (if it be a sin to look upon a woman with desire)
of which this counsel of perfection stands in judgment
upon all men.

He emerges into maturity at the time of his public ministry with a fully developed ethic. His moral standards
must have been hammered out in the interplay of inherited precept of Scripture and the teaching of contemporary rabbis, his own penetrating observations of human
conduct in both aspiration and aberration, and his profound reflection on the meaning of it all under the aspect
of the eternal. We can find counterparts elsewhere of the
individual elements of his ethic. What is original is the
way it is all put together.

And the motivation for goodness of life is fresh: "How
blest are those who know their need of God. . . . How
blest are the sorrowful. . . . How blest are those of a gentle
spirit. . . . How blest are those who hunger and thirst to
see right prevail" (MATTHEW 5:3–6). His is a very positive
approach. One is to be good in order not to miss life here,

now, the more abundant, fulfilling life. The teaching of John the Baptist by contrast marked him as the least in the kingdom. Jesus seems to have been remarkably free of a burdening sense of personal guilt or shame. One can of course account for this in the traditional way by concluding that it reflects his own sinlessness as God incarnate. I reject this as psychologically unacceptable, doing insufficient justice to the humanity of Jesus. I think it reflects, rather, his genuine confidence in the reality and availability of God's forgiveness for the penitent on the one hand and, on the other, the irresistible fascination and allurement which the opportunity for presently living in the kingdom constituted for him.

In Depth Psychological Perspective

One cannot do justice to the human psyche of Jesus without at least making inquiry as to the content and prevailing mood of his own unconscious. What kind of dreams did he have? What was the nature of his "twilight imaging," his waking fantasy? Carl Jung is quite right: we may no longer see any man as merely simplex. Not even Jesus of Nazareth! If he was fully man he too must have been duplex, possessing both a conscious and an unconscious level of being. What went on in the unrecorded unconscious of Jesus? We know he experienced anger and gave expression to it. We know he experienced great sorrow as when, vicariously entering into the grief of Mary and Martha on the death of their brother, Lazarus, it is recorded poignantly, "Jesus wept." We know he experienced fear as when in the Garden of Gethsemane his sweat was, as it were, great drops of blood falling to the ground as he cried, "let this cup pass from me," and when, from the cross he screamed, "My God, my God, why hast thou forsaken me!" We know he experienced searing physical pain in what must be one of its most intense forms, crucifixion. We assume that a man of passion in maturity must have experienced carnal desire in his youth.

What reflection did these human emotions have in Jesus' unconscious, his dreams, and that borderline of the conscious where the unconscious breaks through in fantasy? He lived in a cultural milieu which had traditionally accorded much significance to dreams. Prophets and others had often sought to discern the meaning of dreams, accepting their relevance to, perhaps their compelling message for, life decisions. Jesus lived on the frontier "where the action was" for the Jew of his day. Is it not likely that he experienced nightmares of horrendous proportions?

What were the archetypal images that confronted Jesus in dreams and fantasy? What form did the Jungian "shadow" take in him? Christianity has made much of the concept of the Antichrist. But the shadow that dwelt in the unconscious of Jesus must have been a peculiarly potent form of the antichrist. What images were assumed by his animus and his anima? Again, we raise these questions not because any evidence permits answers, but because the very legitimacy of the questions, once acknowledged, points to and attests the humanity of Jesus.

One can conjecture with some degree of credibility, for example, that the masculine and feminine components in Jesus found extraordinary compatibility and integration. Such must have been the case to permit the kind of stability his personality exhibits in the little we are permitted to know of impressions he made upon those who knew him. The degree to which his own consciousness had been raised with reference to his attitudes toward women is the more remarkable when one recollects the generally accepted male domination within contemporary Judaism, in both cultural and religious institutions.

Moreover, by the same token, there must have been

more integration between his unconscious and his conscious life than is usually realized, for he nowhere exhibits
the telltale symptoms of the driven, compulsive life with
its unconscious projections and false identifications. This
psychic balance, however it came about, must have accounted in part for the sense of "presence" and "whole-
ness" and the resultant power or charisma that shines
through the documents. These characteristics could not
have been "read into" the historic figure. Nor could the
Messiah image have been projected plausibly upon one in
whom these qualities were absent.

As the insights of modern depth psychology began to
accumulate, two inevitable questions arose. First, could
such a figure as Jesus is reported in the Gospels to have
been ever in fact have existed in history? That is to say,
was Jesus in fact a historical figure at all, or was this
figure unconsciously "dreamed up" in response to Old
Testament prophecy and to meet the religious needs of a
particular generation of Jews, hard pressed under Roman
rule? This question of Jesus' historicity has been answered
in the affirmative by those best qualified to respond,
namely historians, applying the best standards of their
own science both to the Gospels themselves and to the
scant references to Jesus in contemporary secular literature.

The second question, characteristic of our post-
Freudian age, is whether such a personality as is depicted
in the Gospel stories could have been fully sane. Must not
anyone reported to have identified personally with the exalted role of Messiah have been suffering some form of
paranoia? Of course a prior question would have to be
resolved: Did Jesus actually think of himself as the Messiah in the senses in which this image is used by those
who are writing of him? Albert Schweitzer, believing that
Jesus did think of himself as the Messiah, undertook as a
physician to defend the sanity of Jesus in a doctoral dis-

sertation entitled *A Psychiatric Study of Jesus*. The main
line of his argument is that Jesus was always totally present in every situation. He always related to reality and
never to an interior aberration out of phase with present
reality, as do the insane. But the question persists, if he
accepted for himself the role of Messiah, to be fully
realized in the impending kingdom, would this not inevitably involve present illusions of grandeur?

From our modern point of view, informed as it is of the
symptoms of paranoia, the question is still a fair one. Individuals with a messianic complex do exist today. It is
usually necessary to institutionalize them. Such a person
lives in an inner world which puts him out of communication with the world about him. If Jesus really believed
himself to be the Messiah, would not this conviction have
precluded normal human communication and relationship? The very fact that the stories do reflect a personality
always "present" and in touch with reality is strong psychological evidence, I believe, that Jesus did not fully
identify with this role, though convinced of his importance in preparing men for the coming kingdom and helping them to enter this realm now. He must have pondered
his role with reference to the Messiah image in contemporary Judaism, but the likelihood is, I believe, that he
did not identify himself with it.

How Did Jesus See His Role?

It is quite clear that he did not identify with that form
of the myth which depicted the Messiah as the Son of
David who would restore the earthly kingdom by crushing the enemies of Israel. The recorded temptation in
which he considered and then deliberately rejected such a
role as presented by the devil is of a piece with the character of the man portrayed throughout the Gospels. Such

a role, assuming it were possible, would have been "out of character." Refusing to accept the role of Son of David for himself, he may well have been deliberately attempting to reshape the traditional myth or to reinforce one version of it through associating power with nonviolence by the manner of his entrance into Jerusalem and by accepting "anointing" from the woman at Bethany.

But what of the Son of Man role as this mythical figure is presented in the books of Daniel and Enoch? Some scholars would hold that this figure is not, strictly speaking, messianic to begin with. But most would agree that while representing a discontinuity with reference to the older myth, one is justified in recognizing this myth as basically messianic in that it also has to do with a supernatural figure sent to redeem the children of Israel and to establish the final kingdom. As to whether Jesus used this epithet of himself there is no consensus among scholars. Bultmann holds, for example, that those sayings in which Jesus speaks of the future work of the apocalyptic Son of Man are to be accepted as authentic *logia*. At the same time he insists that Jesus did not identify himself with that Son of Man but thought of him as someone quite distinct from himself. The critical passages are MARK 8:38, "If anyone is ashamed of me and mine in this wicked and godless age, the Son of Man will be ashamed of him, when he comes in the glory of his Father and of the holy angels," and the variation in LUKE 12:8, "I tell you this: everyone who acknowledges me before man, the Son of Man will acknowledge before the angels of God; but he who disowns me before man will be disowned before the angels of God."

The very fact that Jesus in these sayings appears to distinguish between himself and the Son of Man suggests to Bultmann and those who concur with him that they must be authentic since the post-Easter Church made no such distinction. Others, like Reginald Fuller, feel that

these sayings do not insert another figure between Jesus
and the coming kingdom, but rather, impute to Jesus an
implicit Christology.

Rightly understood, these sayings do not introduce the figure
of the Son of Man for his own sake, but precisely for the sake
of Jesus' own implicit Christological self-understanding. The
Son of Man merely acts as a kind of rubber stamp for the authority of Jesus' own word and person on the final eschatological self-communication of God. In calling men to fellowship
with himself Jesus is giving them already here and now, by
anticipation, the final salvation of the Kingdom of God.[8]

My own feeling is that Jesus probably did not fully and
finally identify himself with the Son of Man image,
though he may have entertained some presentiment along
these lines, but that this is the version of the Messiah
myth which, ideologically, he could approve in principle
as opposed to the Son of David strain. I do not believe
that his ministry itself, where the post-Easter conviction is
not superimposed, reflects a Messiah-consciousness per se.
If he were fully man, as we are assuming throughout, I
believe a sustained Messiah-consciousness would have
taken some aberrant forms which would have offended
the deepest convictions of those about him.

Nothing could so put off a good Jew as the blasphemy
of any claim to be the Son of God. Yet the common people
heard him gladly. The exalted claims recorded in the
Fourth Gospel were imputed to Jesus some seventy years
or so after his death. Peter's purported burst of insight,
"Thou art the Christ, the Son of the living God" may be
authentic in the sense that after the Easter revelation he
recollected an earlier moment of premonition, a not un-
common human experience. But those whose studies have
focused on the assignment of chronology by the scrutiny

[8] Reginald H. Fuller, *The New Testament in Current Study* (New York:
Scribners, 1971), pp. 42–43.

of phrases through Form Criticism have cautioned us against any position of certainty regarding Jesus' personal acknowledgment of Messiah status.

If he did not specifically see himself as Messiah, then how did he understand his role? Clearly he understood himself to be a prophet in the noble succession, but the greatest of the prophets in the sustained quality of his ministry and in the subject matter assigned for prophecy, namely the kingdom of God. He was persuaded that no one had ever understood as well as he the nature of the kingdom as a present interior dwelling place, an enchanting space (to use a contemporary metaphor), in which he habitually found himself, as well as a future earthly abode. His supreme confidence as an interpreter of the kingdom would have appeared arrogant, did it not have a self-authenticating quality about it. He spoke *as one having authority* because it was clear to those who had eyes to see that in the most profound way he practiced what he preached. He knew whereof he spoke because experimentally and existentially he quite clearly lived in the kingdom.

A Recent Development

In his book *The Secret Gospel*, Morton Smith of Columbia University tells the exciting story of finding in 1958 at the monastery of Mar Saba, not far from Jerusalem, a seventeenth-century copy of a letter from Clement of Alexandria in the second century to one Theodore. The letter had to do with a warning about the Carpocratians, one of the Gnostic sects currently practicing a scandalous form of Christianity. But, miraculously, it contained a substantial statement about and quotation from an expanded form of the Gospel of Mark which its author had left to the Church in Alexandria. Clement refers to this

document as a secret Gospel which somehow the Carpocratians had got hold of and were distorting to their own
nefarious ends. The passage directly quoted refers to the
raising from the dead of a youth, the brother of "a certain
woman from Bethany." After six days of private instruction the youth comes to Jesus at night, wearing a linen
cloth over his naked body: "And he remained with him
that night, for Jesus taught him the mystery of the kingdom of God. And thence, arising, he returned to the other
side of Jordan."[9]

When persuaded, after elaborate research and checking
with other scholars, that the document was authentic,
Smith pursued its study with reference to the New Testament and to other contemporary documents and came to
certain, somewhat startling, conclusions. The incident,
like the biblical story of the young man clad only in a
sheet, who disappears into the darkness, naked, when the
sheet is torn from his body, points to a form of baptism
which Jesus himself performed. After careful preparation
for a period, presumably of six days' duration, the candi-
date came clad only in a sheet, prepared for immersion.
But Smith conjectures further that the ceremony, performed in secret, included, unlike John's baptism, an initiation into the "mystery of the kingdom of God." The point
of the ritual practiced by John the Baptist was a cere-
monial washing away of sin, following repentance and
intent to lead a new life. But this baptism by Jesus included, Smith believes, an induced mystical experience of
entering into the kingdom above, where God already
reigned.

Smith interprets this mystical experience as a kind of
"trip" into another space or realm, to borrow a contem-

[9] Morton Smith, *The Secret Gospel* (*The Discovery and Interpretation of
the Secret Gospel according to Mark*), (New York: Harper & Row,
1973), p. 17.

porary metaphor, and relates it to Jesus' own experience at the time of his baptism and to the experience of Paul when he was transported to a seventh heaven, "whether in the body or out of the body (he) knew not." If the disciples had themselves been initiated in a like manner into the mystery of the kingdom, they would have been conditioned to experience the resurrection appearances and the ascension. Like Paul, the initiate would not have been able to distinguish between a spiritual and a physical journey, and hence would have been prepared to believe in a flesh-and-bones resurrection and ascension, given the proper stimuli and associations.

It is a plausible interpretation of the veiled meaning of "the mystery of the kingdom" and would account for the need to conceal the "secret Gospel" since the performer of such a ceremony would no doubt have been persecuted by the Jewish hierarchy and perhaps prosecuted by Roman authorities as well. Smith points out that Jesus was distinguished from other preachers and rabbis in that he shared with other ancient magicians supernatural powers. He lists the following:

the power to make anyone he wanted follow him,
exorcism, even exorcism at a distance,
remote control of spirits and the power to order them about,
giving his disciples power over demons,
miraculous cures of hysterical conditions, including fever, paralysis, hemorrhage, deafness, blindness, loss of speech,
raising the dead,
stilling storms,
walking on water,
miraculous provision of food,
miraculous escapes (his body could not be seized),
making himself invisible,
possessing the keys of the kingdom or of the heavens,
foreknowledge of his own fate, disasters coming in cities, etc.,

knowledge of others' thoughts,

introduction of religious reforms and of new magical rites,

claiming to be united with others, that he is in them and they
in him,

claiming to be a god, or son of god, or united with a god, notably in statements beginning, "I am,"

claiming to be the only one who knows his god, or is known by
his god,

claiming to be the image of the invisible god.[10]

What is important here is not, I think, the extent to which
Jesus made any of these individual claims for himself or
that to which the Gospel writers impute them to him, but
the observation that the claims were common among earlier and contemporary magicians or shamans. In a sense, it
is another testimony to the humanity of Jesus.

We should find it necessary to distinguish between the
mystical and the magical, but not so a contemporary of
Jesus of Nazareth. There is little question that he believed
himself capable of working physical miracles as well as
healing the sick and being transported into another realm,
whether in the body or out of the body. Therefore, in
addition to being a rabbi and prophet, he no doubt
thought of himself as a magician or wonder-worker. But
the important element in these extraordinary powers was
the mystical capacity to identify with the will of God as
he understood it and to transmute this into a life-style
which was immediate and joyous living according to the
moral rule of the kingdom here and now on earth, as a
foretaste and prophecy of the kingdom to come. Though
he won the reputation of a magician, it was as mystic that
he was a spiritual giant and exercised his moral authority
over men.

There was nothing distinctive about the eschatology of
Jesus. He believed, as thousands of his contemporaries

---

[10] *Ibid.*, p. 106.

believed, that the kingdom of God was coming and that it would come by divine fiat. Some believed that the restoration of the kingdom of Israel would come first through a new Son of David sent by God, others that there would be a cosmological cataclysm with God's emissary, the Son of Man, descending from on high to establish the universal reign of God. But, in whatever form, most Jews professed the faith that the coming of the Messiah and the kingdom was imminent. What others did not understand, and what Jesus felt he was sent by God to proclaim, was that one could enter this kingdom now, in spirit and in truth, by following *in the way* and that if one did not respond to this opportunity he would be in danger of forfeiting his citizenship in the outward kingdom when it came. Jesus claimed to be the unique interpreter of a life-style that was itself salvation. His person was not only germane but essential to the whole unfolding eschatological plan. The kingdom to come was already here because he was here. He believed himself to be in some sense necessary to its present and its future manifestations. Therefore his role, if not that of the Messiah, had messianic implications beyond those of prophet in the traditional sense.

This particular assignment as a prophet did indeed have its exalted and transcendent implications therefore, but it was a mission a *man* could fulfill under grace and obedience. It is clear that Jesus also believed that he and his disciples would be reunited at a banquet within the coming kingdom on the other side of death and resurrection. What his role would then be, what relationship he would bear to the Son of Man, these questions, I believe, he was quite prepared to commit into God's keeping. Further there is every indication that he felt the time was short. There is no indication that he anticipated the establishment of a church in the interim which would bear his name and call him Messiah, Son of God.

In Evolutionary Perspective

Just as our depth-psychological perspective helps us to see that Jesus could scarcely have been the effective and persuasive prophet he was, and knew himself to be, had he also been personally convinced that he was the Messiah, so our evolutionary perspective affords us an insight into the mainspring of the extraordinary self-confidence he experienced as a prophet of the kingdom. In the entire evolutionary process, when mutations arise as "sports," they are individual animals of existing species, but distinguished from the others by a precocious development of a physical attribute which incarnates a hidden potential present also in all the others and constitutes the promise of a new species.

Now, man has always had a "within-ness" that bore promise of the capacity for a new life-style which one might call living presently in the kingdom. Suddenly there is a breakthrough on the scale of evolution. Though many men in other cultures and religious traditions have experienced, inwardly, aspects of this kingdom and have been conscious of momentary elevation into its power, in Jesus of Nazareth there was an extraordinary ability to live and breathe in the rarefied atmosphere of this kingdom in a sustained way, without ceasing to be human. Indeed, by becoming more human! It is as if in Jesus man were to have become completely himself, fully "hominized," to borrow a word coined by Teilhard.

We should expect the evolving edge within the species man to be some emerging new form of consciousness. I am persuaded this is the form of consciousness we perceive in the mystics: the capacity to see the world steadily and to see it whole, to perceive relatedness and to experience identification or unity with other men and with the rest of creation and, above all else, with creation's God. My own passionate conviction is that, whatever else he may have been, Jesus was a Jewish mystic, the greatest mystic the world has yet known. He was a "kingdom mystic." His own more intense mystical experiences at baptism and at the transfiguration were experiences of elevation into the kingdom above where the reign of God was already acknowledged. These may have led him to seek to quicken a like experience in others at the time of their baptism into the new faith. This may have been the "secret Gospel" or the experience behind the veiled expression, "the mystery of the kingdom." In any case, the mystical experience of an already existing kingdom above drove Jesus relentlessly to incarnate this kingdom on earth, to establish its moral law here in the relationships between man and man, and to win men to the exhilarating experience of momentary "inbreaks" of this kingdom. This was Jesus' own "realized eschatology." Hence his tireless effort to interpret the nature of the kingdom in parables, in sermons, and in the epistle that was his life.

If symbolically, in harmony with our new evolutionary grasp of reality, we may still call the first man Adam, then Jesus was the second Adam, the new man, the first born, presumably, among many brethren. Must not the first reptile to fly have exulted, however far below the level of sentience, in his newly acquired capacity? How much more, then, a man, empowered with sentience and reflection, must have exulted in the attainment of a new level of being, experiencing life in a new milieu, in a new interior "space." And how inevitably must other men call him Lord and Saviour as they respond intuitively to the incarnation of what they dimly recognize as a potential in themselves, an as yet unlived life.

For man, present salvation, personal and corporate, can now be interpreted as release to become what he has it in him to be, or, to put it another way, to be what he already is by promise. Will he not instinctively call Lord and Saviour one who teaches him of his meaning, tells him who he is, and who he may become? Eckhart speaks of the hidden aristocrat in the depths of every man's being, awaiting the "noble birth in the life of the soul," a birth into the kingdom.

"What happened to Mary," wrote Caryl Houselander, "is precisely what is to happen to each one of us: the Holy Spirit is to conceive the Christ life in us." The mission of Jesus of Nazareth was to convey the reality of this potential. He was indeed the harbinger of the kingdom, its interpreter, and its validation.

The New Wine of the Kingdom

Jesus' life was intoxicated with the heady wine of this unique experience: sustained living in the kingdom. He was passionately constrained to impart this wisdom, and the experience of the life-style itself, to his followers. His energies were consumed in this mission. So certain was he that living in this kingdom was the highest joy a man could know, and so certain was he that his experience was a present inbreak of the kingdom to come, an assurance of its imminent realization, that nothing else mattered by comparison, not even death. Indeed, he began to see that a faithfulness unto death may well be the only way of speeding the coming of the kingdom. The purpose of the Last Supper was to bind himself to his disciples with indissoluble bonds that they might live in anticipation of the kingdom to come as well as sustain its present inbreak as a kind of realized eschatology until he rejoined them in the final eschatological event, the Reign of God on earth.

They are to remember that his life with them has been part and parcel of that kingdom, not merely its present promise. In addition to his parables, by which he had striven to awaken in them a new perception of the kingdom's nature, his very life with them had been a parable openly revealing its secrets to those with eyes to see. In addition to the ethic he had taught, requiring absolute, radical obedience to the will of God, his life-style had confronted them with a foretaste of the kingdom: eating with publicans and sinners, performing healings and exorcisms, and practicing what he preached regarding the need to trust God's providential care, as do the very birds of the air and the lilies of the field. If effective preaching is what Phillips Brooks called it, "truth through personality," then the message of Jesus to his disciples regarding the kingdom reached them most effectively by direct observation of what he was, his life-style, the kingdom style. They were privileged to observe his attentiveness and obedience to the will of God. What they saw with their own eyes made credible the enormous sense of authority implicit in his words and deeds. Early skeptics had been invited to "come and see." Some of them had come and some of these had, indeed, seen.

They had to admit that Jesus knew what was in man because he had revealed to them individually, to an astonishing extent, what was in themselves, of which they had hitherto been unaware. There was no sentimentality in him. He did not see things through rose-colored glasses. He saw the evil in men and stood in judgment upon it. He knew men as sinners. But he stood always ready to forgive and to accept them because he knew also the beauty and goodness that lay hidden in all men and could be released by penitence. And when the disciples sought and found in Jesus the source of his capacity to live in this kingdom that was opening up to them through him they pleaded, "Lord, teach us to pray."

Insofar as Bultmann and the post-Bultmannian scholars have applied the principles of Form Criticism to uncover the earliest stratum embedded in the New Testament, that we may know what we can of the Jesus of history, they have performed a splendid service. Insofar as they have sought to free the existential experience of the good news from forms of mythological interpretation that are no longer acceptable, once again we are deeply indebted. But, insofar as the lines of their own Christology have failed to grasp the importance of, and to follow the curve prescribed by, the perspectives of evolution and depth psychology, they still do not adequately meet our need.

We may agree with Bultmann as a matter of historical observation with regard to the Church that "not the historical Jesus, but Jesus Christ, the preached Christ, is the Lord." But we are constrained to ask a further question. Is it possible any longer for modern man, possessed of the evolutionary and depth-psychological perspectives, either to preach Christ or to respond to the preached Christ in the terms which have been acceptable until now?

It is my conviction that we must distinguish between the historical Jesus and the evolving Christ myth and that we must accept radical revision of the traditional myth if it is to be viable for us today. We must free the central proclamation and demonstration of the Jesus of history about the kingdom from enmeshment in the Christ myth of the kerygma, that he may speak once more to our condition and in order that we may reshape a viable Christ myth for the twentieth century.

We conclude, therefore, that the "whisper" of Jesus' voice and the "outskirts of His ways," as these come through to us in the earliest stratum in the New Testament, thanks to the scholarly application of Form Criticism, can indeed "bear the weight of its post-Easter interpretation in the kerygma" for the disciples, whose world-view was not informed by our modern perspectives. There *was* a "continuous frame of reference between Jesus and the kerygma," or, as we might put it, between the historical Jesus and the Christ myth. However, we of the twentieth century, to whom the Jesus of history still speaks the saving word, but whose world-view has been radically altered, stand under moral obligation to work our way through to a revised kerygma, a new version of the Christ myth which we may profess with the same passionate conviction that characterized the disciples.

III

The birth of the christ myth in the apostolic church

The proclamation of the Jesus of history, as it has been revealed to us by the Form Criticism of the New Testament, is that God was in the process of acting through him and was about to act decisively in the eschatological coming of the kingdom. The proclamation of the Apostolic Church, on the other hand, was that God *had* acted directly and decisively in Jesus. Between the two proclamations lay the crucifixion and the experience of the resurrection.

I say "experience of the resurrection" rather than "resurrection" because I do not believe that a physical miracle of the resurrection of Jesus' body took place. I do believe that for the disciples a decisive *experience* of resurrection did take place, justifying Paul's later observation, "If Jesus be not risen we are of all men the most miserable." I understand the Easter experience of the disciples as a mystical consciousness of the presence in their midst of the Christ they had known in Jesus of Nazareth. Unimpeded by our understanding of the natural world as one world, anticipating always the possibility of the inbreak of the supernatural, (as some perhaps had experienced at baptism), and cherishing traditions in which such a miracle was not unheard of, they leapt to the conclusion, in all sincerity, of a physical resurrection. Presently this appeared substantiated by the report of an empty tomb. Yet it remains inconceivable that a new Israel, calling Jesus Lord and Saviour, could have come into being apart from the motivating power of the resurrection experience.

Looking back upon their life together, the disciples were persuaded that Jesus was indeed the anticipated Messiah, the Christ. This was the only interpretation they could now put upon what they had personally experienced in his earthly presence and what they had just experienced of the risen Christ. They now perceived as implicit in their earthly companionship with him all that the resurrection experiences had made explicit for them. And at once they searched their Scriptures for prophetic anticipation. Further confirmation lay immediately at hand in the Pentecostal experience and in first-hand mystical awareness for individuals of the real presence at baptism and in the Eucharist.

Elements at Work in the Emerging Christ Myth

It is quite clear that the Christ myth had its roots in the Messiah myth and in the way in which the person of Jesus could be related plausibly to certain versions of that myth. It is also clear that the new myth was grounded for the disciples in the resurrection experiences. Now a new element began to emerge in the unbroken, evolving continuity: the kerygma, the kernel of the faith, as it was passionately believed by the disciples, began to be transmitted to others through the phenomenon of preaching.

Here we must understand preaching to be inclusive both of content or message and of personality or life-style. The preachers were not merely proclaimers of "the way"; they were indeed, demonstrably, *those of the way.* As the disciples had initially been drawn to Jesus not merely by what he said but by what he patently *was* as "the way, the truth and the life," so now others were drawn to the disciples by the strange power that had transformed them into "those of the way." The promise that exercised irresistible fascination for growing numbers was that of heightened existence, enhanced personal meaning, and membership in a corporate body that had *eschatological* significance.

Seen in terms of the thesis we shall presently develop, when one's scale of observation is evolution, what was happening was that on the unconscious level men and women were responding to an outward and visible sign of an inward and spiritual grace, deeply rooted in their being. They were drawn to become what darkly and mysteriously they already were by way of inward potential. Jesus had said to his disciples, "You won't know who I am unless the Holy Spirit reveals it to you." Man has evolved to that point where some men will recognize in themselves a kinship with the new man, the first born, and irresistibly respond to become brothers. The Holy Spirit who has been incarnate in the entire process of life from the beginning will now in individual men conceive a noble birth in the life of the soul. The new man is the true aristocrat, a representative of the only aristocracy worthy of our aspiration, the aristocracy of the Spirit.

But of course the process is more complex than this, and rarely pure. In addition to the genuine apostolic succession which takes place by transmission of the charisma from one individual to another, even without "benefit of clergy," as in the baptism by the Spirit of Saul of Tarsus through the faithfulness of the dying Stephen, there is the inevitable human need to formalize the message and to create an institution to channel it. Before the Church became an institution with written documents, spontaneous oral traditions sprang into being and were preserved by teaching and preaching. Presently some of these found their way into written documents that were more or less widely disseminated. Some thirty to forty years after Jesus' death some members of the evolving Church began to feel the need of pulling some of these traditions together in more definitive forms. The evangelists, so-called, the authors of the Gospels, responded to this need, shaping their written accounts with the aid of diverse documents already at hand.

Their purpose, as we have noted, was theological and evangelistic, not biographical or historical in our modern sense. The same was true of the oral and written traditions which had been transmitted to them. It is important that we should also grasp another dimension here. All the authors of the New Testament, whether of documents in their final form as we now have them or of fragments imbedded in these documents, were individual men. Each man was driven by the inescapable and largely unconscious responsibility of articulating in one coherent whole, assimilated by his own unique world-view, the elements of the kerygma as he had received them. This involved inevitable reshaping and additions, however subtle.

So what we must now envision, within the context of the biological space-time, or duration, of what we call the period of the Apostolic Church, is a proliferation of the phylum of the Christ myth into a number of species, if you will, reflecting the stamp of individual creative minds at work upon variations of the same inherited material. When we speak of the evolving Christ myth we must recognize, therefore, a complexity of development that is to characterize it throughout its future, despite the repeated efforts of the Church to freeze this development into creedal statements by its official councils.

Not only can the mainstream of the Christ myth be clearly seen to evolve before our eyes within the time-span of the writing of the New Testament, when we read it with the help of the dating of the various documents by scholars, but we must also recognize that various versions of the myth which did not find their way into the canon also continued to evolve. Already some of these are being judged heretical by the authorities in the Church at the time of the closing of the canon. We see, for example, in the Gospel of John reflections of the existence of such aberrant, docetic forms of the myth by way of the author's condemnation.

Once again, we shall also need to be aware of the principle that, since ideas evolve even as animals in response to changing elements in the environment, those forms of the myth will prove themselves fittest for survival which are most readily assimilated into the prevailing world-views into which they find their way. Other forms will continue to exist wherever intellectual subcultures permit reasonable assimilation. Thus many forms of a myth will survive, even as with animals in the evolutionary process, long after they are naturally relegated to a marginal existence. They then demonstrate their want of vital viability by ceasing to evolve creatively and remaining static or declining into ultimate extinction.

Meantime, every new age, characterized by a distinctively new world-view, however attained, is required to work at reshaping the evolving myth to give it a fresh vitality for contemporary man. This is our present concern. New apologists are demanded by every intellectual revolution "to justify the ways of God to man." However presumptuous the self-appointed assignment may seem, and however time may vindicate or condemn the apologist, his task is undertaken in the name of true religion.

Driven by such motivation, the authors of the New Testament in due course inadvertently submitted their writing for the judgment of history. These books, together with the fragments they contain by other authors, are primarily sermons, or "preachments," written by preachers. The charisma which once accompanied the message in the living preacher comes through in very diluted form, of course. Nevertheless, the objective is as clear as the preached Christ orally presented: conversion.

We shall trace the evolving Christ myth roughly in the order in which these sermons and letters were written, beginning with the authors of the Synoptic Gospels.

Mark's Understanding of Jesus as Messiah

It is the consensus of scholars that the Gospel of Mark was written in the late sixties, not long before the fall of Jerusalem in A.D. 70. By this time there had already been a good deal of development of christological speculation relating to the resurrection experiences. The title for Jesus used most by Mark is "Son of God." But at the same time, for Mark, Jesus is the suffering, dying, rising Son of Man. Now and again he is called the Messiah, as when Jesus asks the disciples, "And you, who do you say I am?" and Peter responds "You are the Messiah" (MARK 8:29). And Jesus himself, when questioned by the high priest, "Are you the Messiah, the Son of the Blessed One?" replies, "I am; and you will see the Son of Man seated at the right hand of God and coming with the clouds of heaven (MARK 14:61–62). Mark reports that at the time of the baptism, the Spirit, like a dove, descended upon Jesus, and a voice from heaven said, "Thou art my Son, my beloved; on thee my favor rests" (MARK 1:11). Again, on the Mount of Transfiguration, "a cloud appeared, casting its shadow over them, and out of the cloud came a voice: 'This is my Son, my Beloved; listen to him'" (MARK 9:7).

Mark deliberately rejects the title "Son of David" as appropriate to Jesus and summons for authority what he reports to have been Jesus' own words:

How can the teachers of the law maintain that the Messiah is "Son of David"? David himself said, when inspired by the Holy Spirit, "The Lord said to my Lord, 'Sit at my right hand until I put your enemies under your feet.'" David himself calls him "Lord"; how then can he also be David's son?

MARK 12:35-37

It is clear that for Mark all titles for Jesus are ultimately inadequate.

He conveys to us the authentic strand of Jesus' own self-consciousness as a prophet, lamenting a prophet's limitation: "A prophet will always be held in honor, except in his home town, and among his kinsmen and family" (MARK 6:4). The central proclamation of this prophet is: "The time has come, the kingdom of God is upon you; repent, and believe the Gospel" (MARK 1:15). Mark sees Jesus as a prophet possessed of supernatural knowledge of things to come. As prophet his self-confidence is supreme in relation to the commission assigned him, that of interpreting the kingdom. His charisma is such that he imperiously commands, and men instinctively respond: "'Come with me and I will make you fishers of men.' And at once they left their nets and followed him" (MARK 1:17). The authority is a delegated one and is exercised on behalf of God. "Whoever receives me receives the one who sent me" (MARK 9:37).

The divine nature is revealed in the power to heal and even more in the power to forgive sins. When the paralytic is lowered to the place where Jesus was and Jesus has said, "My son, your sins are forgiven," Mark reports:

Now there were some lawyers sitting there and they thought to themselves, "Why does the fellow talk like that? This is blasphemy! Who but God alone can forgive sins?" Jesus knew in his own mind that this was what they were thinking, and said to them: "Why do you harbor thoughts like these? Is it easier to say to this paralyzed man, 'Your sins are forgiven,' or to say,

'Stand up, take your bed, and walk'? But to convince you that the Son of Man has the right on earth to forgive sins"—he turned to the paralyzed man—"I say to you, stand up, take up your bed, and go home." And he got up, and at once took his stretcher and went out in full view of them all, so that they were astonished and praised God. "Never before," they said, "have we seen the like."   MARK 2:6–12

This miraculous power extends to the realm of nature. Jesus can rebuke the wind and say to the sea, "Hush! Be still," and they obey at once. He can walk on water; he can multiply loaves and fishes to feed a gathered throng. The disciples are reported as "awe struck," "dumbfounded." Even a Roman centurion is reported to have exclaimed, when he observed Jesus' courage in the face of death, "Truly this man was a Son of God" (MARK 15:39).

Mark was responsible for the notion that Jesus deliberately kept his messiahship a secret. Scholars disagree as to Mark's purpose in infusing this element into his account. Was it an attempt on the part of the earliest evangelist to reconcile the still remembered reticence of Jesus regarding his role with the conviction that he must have known who he was? Was it an attempt to account for Jesus' rejection by many? If historically accurate, was it because Jesus wanted to avoid unnecessary identification in the common mind with the Son of David Messiah role which he could not accept for himself? In any case, Mark stresses the blindness of the disciples: "Their minds were closed" (MARK 6:52). The parables which were obviously intended to interpret and to clarify the nature of the kingdom to the disciples are curiously confessed by Jesus to be a means of confusing the unbeliever:

To you the secret of the Kingdom of God has been given; but to those who are outside everything comes by way of parable, so that (as Scripture says) they may look and look, but see nothing; they may hear and hear, but understand nothing; otherwise they might turn to God and be forgiven.

MARK 4:11–12

Jesus refuses to explain the source of his authority to his enemies. When the chief priests, lawyers and elders demand to know on what authority he acts, Jesus taunts them with a question concerning the authority of John, which they dare not answer, and then coolly concludes: "Then neither will I tell you by what authority I act" (MARK 11:33). Curiously the demons recognize who he is, but this is because they are spirits. "He would not let the devils speak because they knew who he was" (MARK 1:34). Indeed it is they who first identify him: "I know who you are—the Holy One of God" (MARK 1:24). Others say, "You are the Son of God (MARK 3:11).

Despite his already well-advanced Christology, for Mark, Jesus remains human as well as divine. Some have seen in Mark an "adoptionist" idea, that, at the time of Jesus' baptism, he was adopted as son by God. In any case, Jesus' temptations as a man had been genuine. When a stranger addresses him, "Good Master," Jesus rebukes him: "Why do you call me good? No one is good except God alone" (MARK 10:18). He denies that he has the authority to determine who will have favored places in the kingdom: "to sit at my right or left is not for me to grant" (MARK 10:40). He has come to assume the role of servant: "For even the Son of Man did not come to be served but to serve, and to give up his life as a ransom for many" (MARK 10:45). It is not given him to know the day or the hour when the kingdom will come. In his human agony in Gethsemane he prays that the cup might pass from him, but is prepared to receive whatever comes as from the hand of the Father. And even from the cross his last cry is filled with anguish, "My God, my God, why hast thou forsaken me?" (MARK 15:34).

Mark's Gospel, then, is the first extant proclamation of Jesus as the Christ. Mark uses the narrative of Jesus' deeds which have come to him orally to proclaim Jesus crucified and risen. Each story in a measure prefigures the cross. One scholar, W. Marxsen,[1] sees in this work a message to meet a particular situation. The Jerusalem church has fled to Galilee and is awaiting the second coming. Hence the emphasis is not on the resurrection but on the parousia. On the other hand, James M. Robinson[2] sees in the Gospel the unfolding of a drama which Mark believes took place in three acts: preparation in Old Testament until John the Baptist; the earthly ministry of Jesus as a final struggle between Satan and the Son of God, involving the temptations, exorcisms, healings, debates, the misunderstanding of enemies and disciples alike, and the crucifixion; and the present period between the resurrection and the fast-approaching second coming. Mark, in other words, preaches to a congregation under special stress, still awaiting momentarily the advent of the promised kingdom.

Jesus as Ethical Teacher and Prophet in "Q"

Contemporary with Mark, perhaps even a little earlier, but representing an additional source for the authors of Matthew and Luke is a body of transmitted material to which scholars have given the title "Q" (standing for *Quell*, "source"). The unknown author of this material saw Jesus primarily as an ethical teacher and prophet who was in process of bringing in the kingdom. Obedience was the crucial response, not profession of faith by use of exalted title. It will be necessary for the Lord, when he returns, to disown some whose conduct has belied their

[1] W. Marxsen, *Der Evangelist Markus* (Gottingen, 1956).
[2] James M. Robinson, *The Problem of History in Mark* (London and Naperville, Ill.: A. R. Allenson, 1957).

profession of belief: "I do not know where you come
from" (LUKE 13:25). Indeed, "some who are now last
will be first, and some who are first will be last" (LUKE
13:30). Yet Jesus is characterized by compassion. The
parable of the Lost Sheep reflects not only the nature of
God but of his servant Jesus as well. He is primarily concerned to bring the good news to outcasts. If the invited
guests do not come to the wedding feast, the king in one
of Jesus' parables demands: "Go out to the main thor-
oughfares, and invite everyone you can find to the wedding" (MATTHEW 22:9).

A new age has begun with Jesus' presence and his
proclamation of the kingdom. When John, in prison, sends
word, inquiring: "Are you the one who is to come, or are
we to expect some other?" Jesus replies with confidence
that appears almost arrogance: "Go and tell John what
you hear and see: the blind recover their sight, the lame
walk, the lepers are made clean, the deaf hear, the dead
are raised to life, the poor are hearing the good news—
and happy is the man who does not find me a stumbling
block" (MATTHEW 11:3–6). And to sharpen the distinction between the best of the old dispensation and the
new one, the Q material has Jesus say, "I tell you this:
never has there appeared on earth a mother's son greater
than John the Baptist, and yet the least in the Kingdom of
Heaven is greater than he" (MATTHEW 11:11). And
this kingdom is already in their midst. To the questioning
of the Pharisees he retorts, "If it is by the Spirit of God
that I drive out the devils, then be sure the Kingdom of
God has already come upon you" (MATTHEW 12:28).

The disciples are sent forth to prepare the way for his
visitation with the instruction that they themselves are to
proclaim to everyone, "The Kingdom of God has come
close to you" (LUKE 10:9). They are not merely commissioned; they are his surrogates. Failure to respond will be
as damaging as if Jesus himself were present. "Whoever

listens to you listens to me; whoever rejects you rejects me. And whoever rejects me rejects the One who sent me" (LUKE 10:16). The present inbreak of the kingdom has this in common with the future kingdom: immediate and devastating moral judgment. "Whoever disowns me before men, I will disown him before my Father in heaven" (MATTHEW 10:33). Hence there will be much suffering and strife:

You must not think that I have come to bring peace to the earth; I have not come to bring peace but a sword. I have come to set a man against his father, a daughter against her mother, a son's wife against her mother-in-law; and a man will find his enemies under his own roof.   MATTHEW 10:34-35

The author of the Q document accepts the Son of Man metaphor for the Messiah image. Jesus does not hesitate to use it of himself. When a doctor of the law protests he will follow Jesus wherever he goes, Jesus responds, "Foxes have their holes, the birds their roosts, but the Son of Man has nowhere to lay his head" (MATTHEW 8:20). And the disciples are admonished by their Lord, "Hold yourselves ready, then, because the Son of Man will come at the time you least expect him" (MATTHEW 12:40). Jesus thus uses the epithet of himself in the present and in the future sense, and Q thinks Jesus and the anticipated celestial Judge are one.

When Q uses the epithet Son of God he projects a new image of the Messiah, one that might be expected to fall harshly on contemporary Jewish ears. Jesus addressed God thus:

"I thank thee, Father, Lord of heaven and earth, for hiding these things from the learned and wise, and revealing them to the simple. Yes, Father, such was Thy choice." Then turning to the disciples, he said, "Everything is entrusted to me by my

Father; and no one knows who the Son is but the Father, or who the Father is but the Son and those to whom the Son may choose to reveal him."   LUKE 10:21–22

This idea that only the Son knows the Father is not found in earlier or contemporary Judaism. There may be an identification, however, with the Wisdom idea which is present in Wisdom of Solomon, Proverbs, and Ecclesiasticus.

One of the distinctive things about this document is that in it no atoning significance is yet attached to the death of Jesus. Nor is there any indication of what the author feels to be the present status of Jesus after his exaltation in the resurrection and before his anticipated return. The individual's response to the person of Jesus constitutes prejudgment now as when Jesus was on earth. But the significance of the transition between the past and the future, between the earthly Son of Man and the transcendent Son of Man has not yet been thought through.

Jesus as the Expositor of the Torah in Matthew

By the time the Gospel of Matthew was written, more time had elapsed. Since the kingdom had not yet come, there was more concern for the growing institution responsible for the interim transmission of the message. Matthew is the first and only Gospel to use the word *ecclesia,* "church." The Church is becoming more significant because it represents now not merely the faithful awaiting the return of their Lord; it has a growing authority by reason of its expanding responsibility. Authorization for this new power residing in the institution must come directly from the Lord, who is recollected to have said to Peter:

"You are Peter, the Rock; and on this rock I will build my church, and the powers of death shall never conquer it. I will give you the keys of the kingdom of Heaven; what you forbid on earth shall be forbidden in Heaven, and what you allow on earth shall be allowed in Heaven."   MATTHEW 16:18-19

Matthew is concerned for establishing continuities between the earlier ecclesia of the Old Testament period and the present one. Jesus becomes the true expositor of the Torah. Significantly, Matthew has Jesus say to the disciples, when "a teacher of the law has become a learner in the kingdom of Heaven, he is like a householder who can produce from his store both the new and the old" (MATTHEW 13:52). Therefore Jesus is seen as fulfilling prophecy. The beautiful story of the miraculous birth is adduced by the play of imagination upon the Old Testament prophecies concerning Emmanuel, Bethlehem and Galilee. Matthew has the earliest reference to a virgin birth, a new theme in the Christ myth on which Luke will presently play his own variation. Though Mary does not know her husband, Joseph, in the conception, yet the lineage of the child is traced all the way back to David and even Abraham through the father, Joseph. Hence Matthew accepted the Son of David version of the myth as well as the Son of God, the Son of Man, and the Suffering Servant.

Jesus' mission on earth was to Israel, but Israel has rejected him. Therefore a new Israel, a new ecclesia, has been established, one in which righteousness exceeds that of the scribes and Pharisees. Jesus is indeed a second Moses bringing not a new law but the right exposition of the old law. The Church lives under the weight of the impending judgment. The so-called great discourses in Matthew, the sermon on the mount (chapters 5–7), the missionary charge (chapter 10), the parable discourse (chapter 13), the community discourse (chapter 18), and the eschatological discourse (chapters 24–25) spell out the conditions for entrance into the kingdom to come. Matthew has begun a course which Luke will carry further as the little community moves toward the early catholicism realized in the second century. The parable of the Wheat and the Tares stands as a stern warning to members of the ecclesia:

The sower of the good seed is the Son of Man. The field is the world; the good seed stands for the children of the Kingdom, the darnel for the children of the evil one. The enemy who sowed the darnel is the devil. The harvest is the end of time. The reapers are the angels. As the darnel is gathered up and burnt, so at the end of time the Son of Man will send out his angels who will gather out of his kingdom whatever makes men stumble, and all whose deeds are evil, and these will be thrown into the blazing furnace, the place of wailing and grinding of teeth. And then the righteous will shine as brightly as the sun in the kingdom of their Father. If you have ears, then hear.   MATTHEW 13:37–43

One senses in Matthew just a hint of an early ecclesiastical "organization man" and hears the first faint whisper of what later became overt exclusiveness in the dictum: "Outside the Church no one is saved." Yet at the same time nowhere does the moral teaching of Jesus come through in such cogent and sustained monologues that ring true to his character as revealed in the earliest stratum of the New Testament material. It remains true that one begins to feel in Matthew the kind of tightening strictures the counterpart of which General Booth was to lament in his own organization, the Salvation Army, provoking the plaintive query to his wife: "Why is it that God does not allow an organization to remain pure for more than one generation?"

The Evolving Myth in the Hands of the Artist Luke

Writing at a still later date, perhaps around A.D. 90, the author of the Gospel of Luke and the book of Acts reflects yet another step away from the Event and toward the early catholicism of the second century. Though some scholars have questioned that the same person was author of both documents, the consensus at the present time confirms the traditional view. It seems increasingly unlikely that this man was the actual companion of Paul on his missionary journeys, because, as we shall see, on some critical points his views represent a distinct contrast with those of Paul and speak to the condition of a later period of time. Recent post-Bultmannian scholars such as Hans Conzelmann[3] and Ernst Haenchen[4] have pointed to the importance of taking Luke seriously as a theologian in his own right. He is also seen as a literary artist. And while he is not the historian he purports to be in his introduction, he does give us more of an actual life of Jesus than any of the other Gospels.

He has in his possession Mark and the Q source, perhaps more than one travel diary, and other fragmentary documents. But we see the superimposition of one ordering, creative mind upon the materials at hand in terms of summaries, connecting transition material, the way in which he edits the Marcan source, and the composition of some eight speeches put into the mouth of Peter and nine attributed to Paul. He is writing for a new set of circumstances, a new social, political, cultural and theological milieu in the last decade of the first century. As a man of

[3] Hans Conzelmann, *The Theology of St. Luke* (London and New York: Faber and Faber, 1960).

[4] Ernst Haenchen, *Commentary on Acts*, in Meyer series, *Die Apostelgeschicte Kritisch-exegetischer Kommentar* (Göttingen: Vanderhock and Ruprecht, 1954).

letters, he exercises the artist's license to place his own consistent stamp of originality on his interpretive work, of course, but also on his use of sources and recollections.

We see the poet at work, for example, in the beautiful accounts of the annunciation and the birth. It is worth noting that while Luke does not emphasize a virgin birth, he now outdoes Matthew by reciting the lineage all the way back to Adam. The ultimate end of this reading-back will be preexistence. Again the line is traced through Joseph rather than Mary, a curious incongruity if Joseph played no part in the birth. And the boy Jesus in the temple behaves already as the Son of God.

Luke gives some prominence to the Messiah concept that streams from the Son of David tradition. Hence Simeon is described as "one who watched and waited for the restoration of Israel" (LUKE 2:25) and the prophetess, Anna addresses herself to "all who were looking for the liberation of Jerusalem" (LUKE 2:38). Gabriel, in his announcement to Mary, says, "The Lord God will give him the throne of his ancestor David, and he will be king over Israel for ever; his reign shall never end" (LUKE 1:32–33). This would be pure Jewish messianism except that in the same breath the angel says, "The holy child to be born will be called 'Son of God'" (LUKE 1:35). The disciples on the road to Emmaus say to their companion along the way, "We had been hoping that he was the man to liberate Israel" (LUKE 24:21). But the companion responds: "How slow to believe all that the prophets said! Was the Messiah not bound to suffer before entering upon his glory?" (LUKE 24:25–26).

Luke has had access to some special material. We see reflected the early stratum in which Jesus is acclaimed prophet. When Jesus raises from the dead the only son of a widowed mother, the townspeople exclaim, "A great prophet has arisen among us" (LUKE 7:16). And Jesus uses the title of himself when he says to the Pharisees who have warned him of Herod's intent to kill him, "I must be on my way today and tomorrow and the next day, because it is unthinkable for a prophet to meet his death anywhere but in Jerusalem" (LUKE 13:33). Some of the material reflects a fascination by the miraculous for its own sake. There is the story of the extraordinary catch of fish (LUKE 5:8). Jesus is reported to have "watched how Satan fell, like lightning, out of the sky" (LUKE 10:17–20). And he is able to assure the penitent thief from the cross, "I tell you this: today you shall be with me in Paradise" (LUKE 23:43).

Unlike the other synoptic Gospels, Luke frequently refers to Jesus simply as "the Lord" in an unqualified sense. There is the early idea that God has made this Jesus Lord and Messiah: "Let all Israel then accept as certain that God has made this Jesus, whom you crucified, both Lord and Messiah" (ACTS 2:36). Paul is reported to have said in his address in Antioch:

There are now his witnesses before our nation; and we are here to give you the good news that God, who made the promise to the fathers, has fulfilled it for the children by raising Jesus from the dead, as indeed it stands written in the Second Psalm: "You are my Son; this day I have begotten you."

In Acts Luke calls Jesus Saviour as well. When chided by the High Priest for his teaching, he replies: "We must obey God rather than man. The God of our fathers raised up Jesus whom you had done to death by hanging him on a gibbet. He it is whom God has exalted with his own right hand as leader and Savior, to grant Israel repentance and forgiveness of sins" (ACTS 5:31).

Jesus is also seen as servant: "The God of Abraham, Isaac, and Jacob, the God of our fathers, has given the highest honor to his servant Jesus" (ACTS 3:13). Sometimes the epithet has almost a liturgical ring, as in the

disciples' prayer before the rulers, "And now, O Lord,
mark their threats, and enable thy servants to speak thy
word with all boldness. Stretch out thy hand to heal and
cause signs and wonders to be done through the name of
thy holy servant Jesus" (ACTS 4:29–30).

The second coming no longer is considered imminent in
Luke. Rather, though there will still one day be a con-
summation, as predicted, the interim period assumes
greater importance as part of God's redemptive work in
history. The situation has forced assimilation into theology of things as they are. The strain of protracted wait-
ing has been eased. The Church must concern herself
with her mission in the Greco-Roman world in which she
finds herself. Hence Luke illustrates effective missionary
preaching by composing Paul's address to the Athenians
at the Areopagus. We see the principle of adaptation at
work here, accommodation of the kerygma to the congregation. We are aware of striking differences between
Paul's theology and that of his interpreter here. Luke has
made use of what one might call natural theology and
tends to play down the significance of the cross, whereas
Paul had resolved, in retrospect, as he wrote the Corinthians, to "think of nothing but Jesus Christ—Christ
nailed to the cross' (1 CORINTHIANS 2:2–3). Here
Luke is exhibiting the beginning of the kind of art of
apologetics that was to be developed in the second century. Gone in Luke is Paul's emphasis on rejection of the
old law of Judaism in favor of the new law of love. The
speeches imputed to Paul in Acts present Christianity as
the true Judaism. Perhaps we catch here a contemporary
need to win for the new religion certain immunities from
persecution long granted Judaism.

None of the major strands of the variegated Christ
myth has been wholly abandoned, but we continue to observe two central phenomena which are important to our
major thesis: the myth is in process of evolving through

interaction between its inherent potential and the competing world-views in its environment; and the individual creative mind, in this instance Luke's, assimilates and reintegrates the inherited material to accord with his own expanding world-view.

The Christ Mysticism of Paul the Apostle

We come now to Paul. In terms of chronology, some of the authentic epistles would be contemporary with some of the earliest Gospel documents. Yet the thought of Paul influences only the later documents of Luke and John. We see in Paul the impact upon the kerygma of a first-class mind which is driven by a mystical consciousness and a missionary purpose. Albert Schweitzer, in his great study *The Mysticism of Paul the Apostle*, pays tribute to Paul:

Paul vindicated for all time the right of thought in Christianity. Above belief, which drew its authority from tradition, he set the knowledge which came from the spirit of Christ. There lives in him an unbounded and undeviating reverence for truth. He will consent only to a limitation of liberty laid on him by the law of love, not to one imposed by doctrinal authority. . . .[5]

This example, moreover, has great import for our present endeavor:

The result of this first appearance of thought in Christianity is calculated to justify, for all periods, the confidence that faith has nothing to fear from thinking, even when the latter disturbs its peace and raises a debate which appears to promise no good results for the religious life. . . . It is the thoughts of the Apostle of the Gentiles, who was opposed by the faith of his own time, which have again and again acted as a power of renewal in the

---

[5] Albert Schweitzer, *The Mysticism of Paul the Apostle* (New York: Macmillan, 1955), pp. 376–378.

faith of subsequent periods. . . . Christianity can only become the living truth for successive generations if thinkers constantly arise within it who, in the spirit of Jesus, make belief in Him capable of intellectual apprehension in the thought forms of the world-view proper to their time. Paul is the patron saint of thought in Christianity.[6]

We have had occasion repeatedly to recollect that the religious faculty is the compulsion to bind everything together in one bundle. Paul had a very great deal to bind together before he could articulate coherently and in integrated fashion the faith that was in him. On the one hand, he was concerned at the failure of the Jewish community to respond to the preached kerygma and felt inwardly commissioned to become an apostle to the Gentiles. While remaining inescapably a Jew by reason both of birth and of theological training, he felt constrained to interpret the good news in such a way as to make it acceptable to the Hellenistic world-view. This required prodigious intellectual effort.

On the other hand, as a unique individual he had to work out in his own mind a way of accounting, in theological terms, for what had taken place in his own interior experience. This exacted an agony of self-examination, self-understanding and reconciliation of raw experience with the kerygma as it was transmitted to him.

Until conversion, Paul had been a Pharisee of the Pharisees, as he tells us. He had been not merely indifferent; he had been hostile to the new faith. He was driven by a religious zeal to uproot and to cast out this insidious invasion of what he understood to be the faith of his fathers. Meantime he was experiencing a terrible interior conflict. On the one hand, he was striving with might and main to be obedient to the law, which he felt allowed no place for the new doctrine. On the other hand, something

[6] *Ibid.*, pp. 376–378.

in him was irresistibly drawn to the beauty and goodness of the message that was being presented. He had an extraordinary capacity to identify with all men, to be, as he later confided in the new context of his redeemed life, "all things to all men." Hence he was tormented beyond measure.

There is a curious similarity in the inner dynamics of the experience of many of the great mystics. It would appear that as a prelude to their realization of personal unity in the experience of one-ness with the object of their devotion, they must go through a shattering dichotomy that all but tears them to pieces. It is a dark night of the soul more profound than anything they later endure. Then some particular mystical experience resolves the unendurable tension and they become one man, released by what William James called the expulsive power of a new affection.

No man had ever been more divided against himself than Paul. If he could write after conversion, "The good that I would I do not. The evil that I would not that I do," how much more severe must the condition have been beforehand. For one as conscientious as Paul, the law was unendurable in the rigidity of its demands as compared with the frailty of the human will. The more he castigated himself for his failures the more impossible seemed the obedience he demanded of himself. With the fanaticism of a Puritan he was driven to persecute this strange new sect. It infuriated him that this small band of Jews could flout the law with impunity and at the same time be exemplars of a way of life that on another level drew him so profoundly. He was later to understand this terrible stress as "kicking against the pricks."

Especially one young man, Stephen, spoke to Paul's condition through his own transparent witness. Later Paul was a party to the stoning of Stephen. When Stephen emulated his Lord's spirit with his dying words, "Lord, do not hold this sin against them" (ACTS 7:60) the memory of that faith seared its way into the soul of Paul. The crisis came on the road to Damascus in the experience of confrontation by Jesus, "Saul, Saul, why do you persecute me?" He is temporarily blinded but when Ananias is sent to minister to him, the "scales" fall from his eyes and he regains his sight. From that moment on he is a new man. The future pattern of his exhortation to others, "Ye were sometime . . . but now are ye. . . . Put off the old man . . . put on the new man," had its prelude in his own experience. Bultmann's claim that "the salvation event is nowhere present except in the proclaiming, accosting, demanding and promising word of preaching" was of course true of Paul's ministry. But it was also true of his own conversion experience. The preaching of Stephen had been the means of Paul's salvation. At the same time no one would have attached more importance than Paul to the redemptive event itself.

Paul was proud of the fact that he was an apostle, as he was fond of saying, "Not by human appointment or human commission, but by commission from Jesus Christ and from God the Father who raised him from the dead" (GALATIANS 1:1). There had been no official "laying on of hands." Though he had his enemies among the Judaizing Christians, after a time no one seriously challenged his credentials. He tells us of the understanding reached in Jerusalem some fourteen years after his conversion with certain "men of high reputation": "These men of repute . . . acknowledged that I had been entrusted with the Gospel for Gentiles as surely as Peter had been entrusted with the Gospel for Jews. For God whose action made Peter an apostle to the Jews, also made me an apostle to the Gentiles" (GALATIANS 2:6–8).

Paul himself was not a Hellenist. Nor was his gospel Hellenistic. But his articulation of the faith did constitute a bridge to the Hellenistic conceptions which were to be developed by the author of the Fourth Gospel. Jewish eschatological thought remained the context in which the good news was presented. But theological reflection on his own existential experience enabled him to restate the kergyma in such a way that it could speak to the condition of all men. And though we can trace a difference in the later epistles from the earlier ones in terms of the receding intensity of anticipation of the kingdom to come, the manner of entrance into the kingdom now was, throughout, Paul's major original contribution. Christ's death did not accomplish anything automatically for the believer. It is mystical identification with the dying and rising Christ here, now, that works the inward transformation. "I have been crucified with Christ; the life I now live is not my life, but the life which Christ lives with me; and my present bodily life is lived by faith in the Son of God, who loved me and gave himself up for me" (GALATIANS: 2:20).

This potential for new life is not confined to Jews, for whom the death may take the shape it took for Paul: "For through the law I died to law—to live for God" (GALATIANS: 2:19). But others may experience the mystical identity with Christ in other ways. In any case, whatever the interior reference points or associations for the individual: "When anyone is united to Christ, there is a new world; the old order has gone, and a new order has already begun" (II CORINTHIANS 5:17).

This is the earliest Christ mysticism which comes to us in written form. Schweitzer is right, I think, in pointing out that it is not yet God-mysticism. This would have seemed blasphemy to a Jew of Paul's training at that time. It is a "being in Christ," not yet a "being-in-God" as it becomes in John's Gospel. But the greatness of Paul is that his mystical approach to religious experience enabled the gospel to break the bounds of Jewish eschatology in which it had been cast until now and to become available to those disciplined in the Hellenistic world-view. Dying and rising were required by Jewish eschatology for entrance into the kingdom. Now through a mystical identification with Jesus' own death and resurrection the elect need not go through a literal counterpart. ". . . if the Spirit of him who raised Jesus from the dead dwells within you, then the God who raised Christ Jesus from the dead will also give new life to your mortal bodies through his indwelling spirit" (ROMANS 8:11).

The Gentile world was not unfamiliar with sacramental rights at least as practiced in the mystery religions. With Paul the sacraments of baptism and the Lord's Supper keep alive the mystical consciousness which he advocates. Baptism is the sacrament of assurance of personal salvation in the approaching day of judgment. And the Lord's Supper is not merely a memorial of the feast in the upper room; it is an anticipatory celebration of the messianic feast which is mystically experienced here, now: "For every time you eat this bread and drink the cup, you proclaim the death of the Lord, until he comes" (I CORINTHIANS 11:26). So while the eschatological element is preserved, the immediacy of the mystical experience makes it palatable for the Gentile mind. Paul's genius is revealed in the synthesis he has achieved. What he has pulled together are the warring members in his own psyche, elements of the Messiah myth he has inherited from Judaism, and penetrating insight into the need of an alien people for a living faith. The motive power of compassion has been ignited in him by Paul's own mystical experience: "I, yet not I, but Christ in me." A way of life has been freed by Paul from its moorings to Judaic cultic practice; it is set free to sail the high seas in quest of unvisited human harbors. The Greek Gentile can respond to a person who symbolizes a life-style when he would be put off by laws and doctrines and cultic practices that have not been part of his own milieu.

As we develop the thesis to which we are committed here, we shall see that it is the central mystical strain in Paul's own experience that constitutes the universal element, transferrable to and assimilable by other world-views, including our own. As Schweitzer puts our mandate, once again:

It is the thoughts of the Apostle of the Gentiles, who was opposed by the faith of his own time, which have again and again acted as a power of renewal in the faith of subsequent periods. ... Christianity can only become the living truth for successive generations if thinkers constantly arise within it who, in the spirit of Jesus, make belief in Him capable of intellectual apprehension in the thought forms of the world-view proper to their time.[7]

This does not mean that we need to adopt Paul's peculiar form of Christ mysticism. It does mean that we may be challenged by Paul to help do for our day what he did for his: to dedicate our thinking capacity and our mystical faculty to the realization of a synthesis that at once preserves continuity and makes the essence of the faith viable for a new day. Paul demonstrated that the essence of the kerygma is that the law of love revealed in Jesus' way abrogates every other law.

And this discovery is not a mystical experience for its own sake. The mysticism of Paul the apostle is an ethical mysticism making prodigous moral demands of its devotee. There is in some circles today a tendency to contrast the prophetic and the mystical elements in religion. There is no dichotomy here. Insofar as religion is genuinely mystical, it is inevitably prophetic. It is the very experience of identification that is the most profound and abiding motivation for social reform. Only the mystic can

[7] Albert Schweitzer, *The Mysticism of Paul the Apostle* (New York: Macmillan, 1955), pp. 376, 378.

say with conviction: "Who suffers, and I do not suffer?"
Only in the mystic is passion transmuted into compassion
by the alchemy of love. "For the whole law can be
summed up in a single commandment: 'Love your neigh-
bor as yourself'" (ROMANS 13:9).

In his earliest letters Paul is concerned with the second
coming which is conceived as imminent: "To wait expec-
tantly for the appearance from heaven of his Son Jesus" (I
THESSALONIANS 1:10); "at the word of command, at
the sound of the archangel's voice and God's trumpet-call,
the Lord himself will descend from heaven" (I THES-
SALONIANS: 4:16).

Paul often uses the word "Christ" as if it were Jesus'
surname, but he also prefixes it to Jesus as a title and
sometimes uses the title as a substitute for the name. But
he radically reinterprets the title to make it inclusive of
elements not anticipated in the Old Testament. For
example:

. . . but we proclaim Christ—yes, Christ nailed to the Cross;
and though this is a stumbling-block to Jews and folly to
Greeks, yet to those who have heard this call, Jews and Greeks
alike, he is the power of God and the wisdom of God.

I CORINTHIANS 1:23–24

This involves a wisdom which the worldly cannot comprehend:

The powers that rule the world have never known it; if they
had they would not have crucified the Lord of glory.

I CORINTHIANS 2:8

This wisdom has accounted for the strange paradox:

For you know how generous our Lord Jesus Christ has been:
he was rich, yet for our sake he became poor, so that through
his poverty you might become rich.   II CORINTHIANS 8:9

The identification of the believer with his Lord makes inward revelation possible:

For the God who said, "Out of darkness let light shine," has caused his light to shine within us, to give the light of revelation—the revelation of the glory of God in the face of Jesus Christ.   II CORINTHIANS 4:6

The humanity of Jesus is emphasized in pointing to the weakness on the cross. If the disciples will identify with this "weakness" they may exercise the same power.

True, he died on the cross in weakness, but he lives by the power of God; and we who share his weakness shall by the power of God live with him in your service.
                    II CORINTHIANS 13:14

The humbling of himself is set in contrast to the ultimate glorification:

Bearing the human likeness, revealed in human shape, he humbled himself, and in obedience accepted even death— death on a cross. Therefore God raised him to the heights and bestowed on him the name above all names, that at the name of Jesus every knee should bow—in heaven, on earth, and in the depths—and every tongue confess, "Jesus Christ is Lord," to the glory of the God the Father.   PHILIPPIANS 2:8–11

The Christology mounts in the later epistles to cosmic dimensions:

For it is in Christ that the complete being of the Godhead dwells embodied.   COLOSSIANS 2:9

He is the image of the invisible God; his is the primacy over all created things. In him everything in heaven and on earth was created, not only things visible but also the invisible orders of thrones, sovereignties, authorities and powers. The whole universe has been created through him and for him. And he exists before everything and all things are held together in him.

COLOSSIANS 1:15–17

So in Paul are all the elements in the Jesus of history integrated into one harmonious whole: his humanity revealed as ethical teacher and healer with the divinity expressed as Messiah, Son of Man, Son of God, Wisdom of God.

Jesus as the Incarnate Logos in John

Though the Gospel of John was probably not the latest of the books of the New Testament to be written, it does represent the most advanced point in the development of Christology. It is not that there is one single line pursued by the evolving myth, but that all the major developments, including the Pauline, are presupposed by John. Yet, like Paul, the author of the Fourth Gospel put the stamp of his own originality on his work.

But who is this author? His identity has long been in dispute. Very early tradition, beginning with Irenaeus, attributed this work to the apostle John, the son of Zebedee. As important contemporary figures as William Temple and Charles Raven have supported the tradition. More recent consensus regarding the dating of the Gospel has moved it forward from 125–135 to around 100. This would tend to substantiate the claim because, while the apostle would have been a very old man, it is within the realm of possibility that he could have written it.

The more generally accepted view on the part of scholars today is that it was not written by the apostle. Some hold that it was written by a disciple or follower of John the apostle, namely John the elder in Ephesus. Whether the apostle is the author or the one who inspired another to write it, and thus stands in some sense behind the Gospel, some such identification between John, the son of

Zebedee, and the burden of this message would make impressive psychological sense. It would account for the veiled references to the "beloved disciple." There would be motivation for insisting upon anonymity while witnessing to the transforming experience on the part of one reminiscing many years after the event. If this paeon of praise to the gospel of love was written by one of the two "sons of thunder" who had pleaded with the Master to rain down fire from heaven upon the inhospitable Samaritans and had sought on their own behalf, as well as through the importunity of their mother, favored places at the banquet table in the approaching kingdom, it becomes especially understandable why love should be the central theme in the reiteration of the good news. Clearly these two may well have been initially the least lovable of those Jesus drew to him. Only one capable of loving the unlovable could have transformed such a one as John into the mature exponent of the way of love set forth here. Yet such a miracle would have been possible for the man Jesus, living in the kingdom whose nature and power he demonstrated for those about him.

But while there is profound poetic truth in this possibility, it must remain, perhaps forever, pure conjecture. Some reputable scholars reject both of the above theories and simply attribute the Gospel to an unknown author at the close of the first century. There is growing consensus, however, that he was a Palestinian Jew familiar with the topography of that area as well as certain emphases within rabbinical Judaism and that he was also conversant with contemporary Hellenized Judaism and with Gnosticism whether of the Hellenistic or more occult oriental form, as Bultmann believes.

His central purpose, as he tells his readers, is "that you may believe that Jesus is the Christ, the Son of God, and that through this faith you may possess life by his name" (JOHN 20:31). It is true, as has often been pointed out,

that he seems in addition to have three incidental purposes: to condemn the Jews for their hostility to Jesus, to
discredit a contemporary sect which still hallowed the
memory and proclaimed the message of John the Baptist,
and to answer false teachings about Jesus currently disseminated by a form of Gnosticism known as Docetism
by skillfully adapting and assimilating some aspects of the
teaching while rejecting others.

But the central motivation remains the compulsion to
share the inwardness of his own experience as he has
reflected upon and integrated its relevance within his
own world-view. He wants to make this experience available to a new age and to persons living in a new cultural
and intellectual climate. With Paul he shared the honor of
being a great apologist for the Faith. In common with the
recently discovered Dead Sea Scrolls, this author is fond
of juxtaposing opposites, as with Gnosticism, but with the
characteristic Old Testament insistence that God is the
creator of good and evil alike. There remains ethical and
eschatological dualism, but thorough-going theological
monotheism.

More individuals within the continuity of Christian
piety have accorded first place to this book in preference
to any other in its capacity to reach the heart and to
persuade the mind. William Temple called it the "pro-
foundest of all writings." W. A. Smart said of it: "More
people have gone to these few pages for strength and
comfort in life's hard places, for deep and abiding faith,
and for thrilling assurances of the presence of God in their
lives, than to any other single writing ever penned."[8]
Luther called it "the chiefest of the Gospels." Recently
C. K. Barrett has said of its author that he was "perhaps

8 W. A. Smart, *The Spiritual Gospel*, (Nashville: Abingdon-Cokesbury,
1945), p. 134.

the greatest theologian in all the history of the church."⁹

What, then, are the distinctive contributions of this author to the evolving Christ myth? What are the elements in the tradition that he pulls together in his own unique way into a unity harmonized with new elements in the ongoing process? He uses the titles "Messiah," "Christ," "Son of God." Nathanael uses three titles all at once: "Rabbi, you are the Son of God; you are king of Israel" (JOHN 1:49) reflecting three traditions. Jesus accepts the exalted epithet. After the foot-washing ceremony, Jesus says to the disciples: "You call me 'Master' and 'Lord,' and rightly so, for that is what I am" (JOHN 1:13). When Thomas exclaims, "My Lord and my God!" Jesus makes no disclaimer, but responds "Because you have seen me you have found faith. Happy are they who never saw me and yet have found faith" (JOHN 20:28–29).

But "Son of God" has now an accumulated weight of meaning. Jesus is portrayed as well aware "that he had come from God and was going back to God" (JOHN 13:3). What was implicit in earlier Gospels has become explicit in such references as "not born of any human stock, or by the fleshly desire of a human father, but the offspring of God himself" (JOHN 1:13). He is contrasted with the greatest of his predecessors: "Law was given through Moses, grace and truth come through Jesus Christ. No one has ever seen God; but God's only Son, he who is nearest to the Father's heart, he has made him known" (JOHN 1:18). The preexistence is stressed. John the Baptist says of him, "This is the man I meant when I said, 'He comes after me but ranks before me'; for before I was born, he already was" (JOHN 1:15). When the Jews protested his claim that Abraham was overjoyed to see his

⁹ C. K. Barrett, *The Gospel according to St. John* (London: S.P.C.K., 1955), p. 1136.

day, "You are not yet fifty years old. How can you have seen Abraham?" his rejoinder is: "In very truth I tell you, before Abraham was born, I am" (JOHN 8:58).

He does his Father's work in the world, and is accused of claiming equality with God. He calls upon the Father to glorify his name in him. He is reported to use the title "Son of Man" of himself in the context of such glorification. "In truth, in very truth I tell you all, you shall see heaven wide open, and God's angels ascending and descending upon the Son of Man" (JOHN 1:51). Now the title has sacramental significance: "This food the Son of Man will give you, for he it is upon whom God the Father has set the seal of his authority" (JOHN 6:27). "In truth, in very truth I tell you, unless you eat the flesh of the Son of Man and drink his blood you can have no life in you" (JOHN 6:53). Even those who have not embraced the faith as true believers can exclaim, as the Samaritans, "We know that this is in truth the Savior of the world" (JOHN 4:42). Or some of the people on another occasion, "This must certainly be the expected prophet" (JOHN 7:40).

The Suffering Servant idea is brought forward in such a way as to anticipate its liturgical significance. John the Baptist exclaims, "Look, there is the Lamb of God; it is he who takes away the sins of the world" (JOHN 1:29). Moses had been the lawgiver but Jesus does not hesitate to proclaim, "I give you a new commandment: love one another; as I have loved you, so you are to love one another" (JOHN 13:34). Jesus' teaching largely relates to faith in himself, which is essential to salvation: "God loved the world so much that he gave his only Son, that everyone who has faith in him may not die but have eternal life" (JOHN 3:16).

But the most distinctive emergent in John is the fusion of the Greek Logos concept with the Hebrew Messiah concept. Scholars have not been able to demonstrate that John was influenced here by the way in which Philo, an

Alexandrian Jewish philosopher used the word *logos*, but Philo's ideas were current in the contemporary world. Philo undertook to account for the relationship between God and the world by means of this idea. Logos is, variously, the beginning of the world, God's eldest son, and his first born. The Logos was created by God along with the ideas which constitute the archetypes of all things. Logos represents a mediator between God and man. In Philo's mind there was a close relationship between Moses and *logos*. But Logos is never an independent person. So there are parallels here, but important differences.

John's "Logos" was with God at the beginning and was the agent of creation itself. His life, moreover, infused all life and has constituted the light of men. "All that came to be was alive with his life, and that life was the light of men" (JOHN 1:4). This Logos was Jesus himself. "So the Word became flesh; he came to dwell among us, and we saw his glory, such glory as befits the Father's only Son, full of grace and truth" (JOHN 1:14).

The Logos concept picks up and develops the idea of Colossians and Hebrews that the Christ was the agent of creation. The emphasis now, however, is on the agent's involvement in the process of redemption and revelation. Though the Logos was with God from the beginning it is also implied that he *is* God. He speaks for God, "for he whom God sent utters the words of God" (JOHN 3:34), does God's work, "My Father has never yet ceased his work, and I am working too' (JOHN 5:17), is indeed one with God, "My Father and I are one" (JOHN 10:30). The development of the Christ myth has reached the point of the declaration of the full divinity of Jesus.

There are certain parallels in Gnostic redeemer-myths which were current. Some of the images are the same as those of the Mandaean literature: bread of life, water of life, life, truth, way, vine, shepherd, door, gate. But in John there is no separation between the creator and the redeemer. It is emphasized that they are one. Men stand in need of redemption but not of a new creation. The original creation continues to remain the object of God's love. Moreover, no Gnostic redeemer was ever represented as fully human. John's redeemer, the Logos, however divine and one with God, assumed flesh and lived with man, is reported as having shared aspects of the human condition of men including weariness, thirsting, suffering, and death.

Yet, on the whole, divinity is stressed more than humanity, which after all has only been temporarily assumed for a purpose. The vision of Paul of a risen and glorified Christ is now read back into the earthly life. In his own distinctive way John interprets present living in the kingdom as the reward of belief in the divinity of Jesus which bestows immortality here and now. And the earthly life is expanded to suggest that Jesus' mission from the beginning was addressed to Samaritans and Greeks as well as Jews.

Jesus reflects other attributes of divinity. He has supernatural knowledge which can see Nathanael clairvoyantly under a fig tree before he comes. "He knew men so well, all of them, that he needed no evidence from others about a man, for he himself could tell what was in a man" (JOHN 2:25). He knew the background of the Samaritan woman at the well before she confessed it to him. And he knew that betrayal would come and who would be its perpetrator. Communication with his father is instantaneous and sustained in ways that others cannot comprehend: "Father, I thank thee; thou hast heard me. I knew already that thou hearest me, but I spoke for the sake of the people standing round, that they might believe that thou didst send me." (JOHN 11:42)

Jesus does not pray to be spared the death. He has foreknowledge of it. Before Pilate in response to the direct query, "You are a king, then?" he makes equivocal reply:

" 'King' is your word" (JOHN 18:37), but he implies that "My kingdom does not belong to this world. If it did my followers would be fighting to save me from arrest by the Jews. My kingly authority comes from elsewhere" (JOHN 18:36–37). Though the powers of evil appear to have their way, Jesus is in command throughout: "I lay down my life to receive it back again. No one has robbed me of it; I am laying it down of my own free will. I have the right to lay it down and I have the right to receive it back again" (JOHN 10:17–18). It is he himself who must give permission for the arrest. And in sharp contrast with the last word of Jesus as reported in Mark, "My God, my God, why hast thou forsaken me?" there is the cool detachment of the pronouncement, "It is accomplished" (JOHN 19:30).

For all the doctrinal enrichment of the myth contributed by this author, I believe that the chief value of this Gospel is that it is a great mystical document, indeed, as Inge calls it, "the charter of Christian mysticism."

Its author ranks with Paul among the first and greatest in what might be called the apostolic succession of the Christian mystics. The genius of the Gospel is its mystical insight. Scholars have only recently concluded that in certain important matters such as the date of the last supper and crucifixion with reference to the Passover, this Gospel may well be more accurate than the synoptics. But more important still, the portrait we have of Jesus in this Gospel, despite the much greater distance in time from the original and the consequent elaboration of pious imagination both of words and deeds as well as of doctrinal development, may be truer to life in one all-important respect: Jesus himself comes through as a Jewish mystic, perhaps the greatest mystic of all time.

The only begotten son of the Father is convincingly revealed, if inadvertently, as the first born of many brethren in this most important respect. It takes a mystic to understand and to interpret a mystic. Even though we are much further from the event here, I believe we are much nearer the man, Jesus, in the inwardness of his self-consciousness. But this apparently presumptuous claim will take careful interpretation.

Jesus is revealed here as a kingdom mystic, or God mystic. Paul never went beyond a being-in-Christ mysticism. John realizes a being-in-God mysticism and imputes the same experience to Jesus. Whereas Paul can say out of his genuine mystical experience, "I, yet not I, but Christ in me," what Jesus seems to be saying by implication over and over again in this Gospel is, "I, yet not I, but God in me." This, symbolically, is the immediacy, the inwardness, of Jesus' experience.

When Jesus is reputed to have said, "Anyone who has seen me has seen the Father" (JOHN 14:9), though the claim would seem blasphemous in the mouth of a lesser man, it is nevertheless precisely what other great mystics have claimed. When Meister Eckhart in a moment of mystical ecstasy blurted out (and was posthumously excommunicated for it) "My me is God," he was saying basically the same thing. Most of the great mystics have reported this inner assurance of identification in unity with deity, by whatever name they called their God. Therefore I think the phenomenon we are observing here, while, on the one hand, it reflects the peak of theological development of the Christ myth in the New Testament, at the same time, quite unconsciously, and perhaps accidentally, it very accurately reflects what in all probability was the inner self-awareness of Jesus as a Jewish mystic.

It is not only that Jesus may well have felt the kind of identity with the mind and will of God attributed to him here, without accepting for himself epithets this author bestows on him. It is clear that he did in fact think of himself as anticipating the approaching kingdom in present realization. While he may never have spoken the words, "I am the way, I am the truth, and I am life" (JOHN 14:16), everything we know of him from the earliest stratum of the synoptics indicates he must have believed all that is implied in them to be true of himself. Certainly he believed that he alone among men had been privileged to enter into the life-style of the kingdom to such a depth and in such a sustained way.

And it is important to realize that for Jesus to have been convinced that he had experienced unity with a Father-God in spirit and in deed and that he had happened on a way of life, by the grace of God, that was indeed a fore-taste of the kingdom, is quite different from having been convinced that he was the Messiah, the Son of David, the Son of Man, the only Son of God.

It is hard to see how the latter set of convictions could have been harbored, even by the Jesus of history, whose life has subsequently borne their weight more than any other could have, without producing paranoia. The former set of convictions stand under no such indictment, and are not merely plausible but highly probable. Indeed this would make sense of much that otherwise seems inexplicable in the account.

This being-in-God, which Jesus experienced as a mystic and which John also experiences and interprets in metaphors appropriate to his world-view at the close of the first century, is available to any believer. John's self-appointed mission is to interpret this "way." Paul had advocated a Christ mysticism in which the Spirit is bestowed on the believer by experiencing a dying and rising again with Christ through mystical identification with him. This process produced a being-in-Christ, a participation in his present resurrection state. In this way, Paul had built a bridge from Jewish eschatology to the Hellenistic mind.

But John went further. He did not make use of the dying-and-rising metaphor, nor was the mystical objective

for him a being-in-Christ. With early church fathers Ignatius and Polycarp, John saw the Spirit as inherently
present in the natural man, however separated it might be
from the flesh. Hence the present resurrection state is
achieved not by doing away with the flesh, as in Paul, but
by transforming it. The flesh and the spirit in the believer
are to be united as the divine and human were united in
Jesus. This is realized through mystical union with Christ
in the sacraments. We perceive here a shift in emphasis
from the death and resurrection of Jesus to the incarnation. Concurrently there is a shift from emphasis upon
baptism to emphasis upon the Lord's Supper. And the
objective of the mystical experience is not being-in-Christ
but being-in-God.

The symbolism of baptism and the Lord's Supper is
adapted to the new world-view. Baptism by the Spirit as
well as baptism by water is now required. There is the
notion of rebirth, the second birth providing for the believer an opportunity for the union of flesh with Spirit
which took place at the incarnation, Jesus' own birth. This
union will then be sustained and nourished through the
sacrament of the Lord's Supper, for when the sacrament is
performed the Spirit is mystically present in the symbols
of the body and blood of Christ.

During Jesus' life on earth, the Spirit, that is, the Logos,
had been confined to him. But he had taught his disciples
that when he went to the Father, the Spirit would come to
be with them. Henceforth they were to constitute an
"apostolic succession" by which the Spirit was to be made
available to the others through the sacraments. Hence,
after the resurrection, in John, Jesus is reported as infusing the disciples with the Spirit:

Jesus repeated, "Peace be with you!" and said, "As the Father
sent me, so send I you." Then he breathed on them, saying,
"Receive the Holy Spirit." If you forgive any man's sins they

are forgiven; if you pronounce them unforgiven, unforgiven they remain.   JOHN 20:21–23

The mystical union with God the Spirit is maintained through the sacrament: "Whoever eats my flesh and drinks my blood dwells continually in me and I dwell in him. As the living Father sent me, and I live because of the Father, so he who eats me shall live because of me" (JOHN 6:56–57). Thus the Spirit will continue to unite with the elements in the Lord's Supper even as the Logos Spirit had united with water, flesh, and blood in the body of Jesus at the incarnation. Through the sacraments the disciples are not only joined with Christ in mystical union but also with the Logos as he had been joined at birth; hence with God. Moreover, since Jesus has entered upon the resurrection state the disciples through this union attain the resurrection state here, now, with him.

In John, the parables, as Jesus' means of teaching about the kingdom, are replaced by certain signs or miracles which, understood as allegories, represent the stamp or seal of the kingdom and are intended to impart spiritual truth about the kingdom. Miracles are recounted as still more miraculous, as for example the blind man is said to have been *born* blind and it is specified that the walking on water took place twenty-five to thirty furlongs from shore. All of these signs or wonders have a spiritual message to impart beyond the immediate event. When water is turned into wine it is to be remembered that to be with Jesus introduces joy, a kind of intoxication, into life. If Jesus could heal the paralytic let it be remembered that he can also heal the paralyzed soul. When the man born blind is made to see, those standing about are reminded that: "It is for judgment that I have come into this world —to give sight to the righteous and to make blind those who see" (JOHN 9:39).

And when Lazarus is raised from the dead, an extraordinary miracle for the synoptics to omit, Jesus drives the message home: "I am the resurrection and I am life. If a man has faith in me, even though he die, he shall come to life; and no one who is alive and has faith shall ever die." (JOHN 11:25)

Jesus was the "resurrection" even before he died. Hence it is possible through mystical union with him now to participate in the resurrection life at once. Similarly the eschatological future event of the kingdom is transposed into present reality. Jesus the kingdom mystic, understood and interpreted by John the mystic, makes entrance into the kingdom an immediate fact of experience for all who will respond to the invitation to embark upon this mystical union with God in the Christ, through faith. Moreover, deep within the believer himself is the touchstone for verification: "Whoever has the will to do the will of God shall know whether my teaching comes from him or is merely my own" (JOHN 7:17).

The disciples are to enter into a symbiotic relationship with Jesus the Christ symbolized by the vine and the branches: "Dwell in me as I in you. No branch can bear fruit by itself, but only if it remains united with the vine; no more can you bear fruit, unless you remain united with me" (JOHN 15:4).

And this union of course extends to the Father as well, so that Jesus may pray:

As Thou, Father, art in me, and I in thee, so also may they be one in us that the world may believe that thou didst send me. Thy glory which Thou gavest me I have given to them, that they may be one, as we are one; I in them, and they in me, may they be perfectly one. Then the world will learn that thou didst send me, that thou didst love them as thou didst me.

JOHN 17:21-23

So are we called to the very being-in-God which was the core of Jesus' own mystical experience!

IV

The evolution of the christ myth in history

It will not be possible, within the compass of this book, to trace all of the various strands of the Christ myth as they continued to evolve, or to remain static, with reference to the changing world-views by which they were confronted. It should be helpful, however, before presenting in the last chapter a form of the myth I believe to be viable for the modern man whose mind has been informed of the findings of evolution and depth psychology, to suggest the way in which the myth continued to interact with the philosophical and psychological environment in which it found itself.

We shall first review in outline the early church period during which the myth was still growing by accretion and assuming its final and classic form in the creeds of the Church.

Then we must consider those radical changes in the philosophical and psychological climate in the seventeenth and eighteenth centuries that were occasioned by rationalism and the inductive process of scientific inquiry. These ultimately produced a world-view in which, for many, the Christ myth would no longer survive in any recognizable form.

Finally, it is important to recognize that one strand of organic continuity in the Church, what we have called the apostolic succession of the mystics, was able, through the form of empiricism to which it was already committed (namely, continuing revelation through first-hand religious experience), to survive the shaking of the foundations. The mystics retained the core and spirit of the myth by allowing it to continue to evolve. Orthodoxy has held fast to the primitive myth, but only at the expense of operating with a divided mind, applying deductive reasoning to unchallenged, ancient revelation, embraced by a leap of faith, and inductive reasoning in areas of scientific inquiry. But the mystics have been able to keep their world one, "to see life steadily and to see it whole," and have thereby been more faithful to the religious instinct itself: getting it all together.

I.   Early Church Debate on the Two Natures of Jesus

Prevailing Cultural and Religious Milieu

During what has often been called the patristic epoch, from apostolic times until the middle of the fifth century, the creeds which are still recited in the churches were being shaped by the all-inclusive ecumenical councils. The Church, meantime, was suffering sporadic persecution and its energies were consumed in struggling for its identity in opposition to Gnostic movements which threatened not merely to modify its basic doctrines, but to transform them. At the same time, it was a period of creative controversy in which the Christ myth was exposed to new and evolving world-views, and issues raised in the attempt at viable integration were resolved in such a way as to leave an indelible stamp on subsequent developments.

It was a period of restive change, which witnessed the further dissolution of ancient religions and the rise of new religions, a time within the Greco-Roman world of the death of the gods and the proclamation of new gods. All was in flux, culturally and intellectually, and it was a question, as always within the process of evolution, of the survival of the fittest: the fittest, that is, in terms of assimilation, adaptation, and relevance to the needs of contemporary man.

While the growing spirit of nationalism found it convenient to require worship of the emperor with varying degrees of intensity, according to the demands of the incumbent, this official state religion did not meet the religious needs and aspirations of reflective and sensitive men and women. For the average man, it served as a symbol of corporate solidarity and afforded comfort as against fear of invasion from without, but it could not provide nutriment for the undiscouragable upreach of the religious aspiration for holiness of life and present mystical experience. The oriental cults that had begun to spread throughout the Greco-Roman world in the century before Jesus spoke to this condition. For many, Isis, Mithras, Serapis, and Cybele were replacing the gods of the Greek and Roman pantheons.

In other circles, the prevailing polytheism of the classical period had been superseded by a new monotheism which sought to establish continuity by maintaining that the gods of the pantheon were personifications of the various attributes of the one god, or differing manifestations of the activities of his power. The current mood fostered syncretistic development of all kinds. The celebrated biographer Plutarch could allow for the existence of gods and demons while acclaiming the supremacy of the one true god. And the emperor Aurelian in 274 could introduce the state cult of Sol Invictus, not only to encourage the chauvinistic spirit, but to make it palatable by symbolizing in this way the one universal god.

Contemporary Philosophical Schools

It was particularly the philosophical ideas, permeating

the prevailing culture, that constituted the intellectual milieu with which the evolving Christ myth would have to come to terms, if it was to survive. The three principal schools of thought were Platonism, a contemporary form of skepticism, and Stoicism.

Plato had taught that knowledge is possible because of the existence of a transcendent, nonmaterial world of forms and ideas, which can be apprehended by the intellect. The mind has the capacity to discern what characteristics individual objects have in common. These comprise the forms which Plato arranged in a hierarchy whose summit was the most universal form, the form of the Good, or the One, the source of all other forms. Only forms are ultimately real.

The human soul is itself a form whose existence antedates its present incarnation. The soul, in turn, is itself comprised of three elements: the "rational," which, because it is capable of apprehending truth, should remain in control of the others; the "spirited," which is the spring of the finer emotions; and the "appetitive," which is the source of carnal desires. There is also a World-Soul presiding over the material universe which comes closer in Plato to the counterpart of the Judeo-Christian God than the form of the Good or the One, who would more nearly correspond to the Godhead in later Christian theological development.

Aristotle had modified his mentor's concepts and introduced some of his own. He insisted that the mind organizes its thought through what he called categories: substance, quantity, quality, relation, place, data, position, state, action, passivity. These also constitute the modes or states in which sensible matter exists. In comparison with Plato, he was therefore a materialist. The forms, he insisted, do not exist apart from the substance of things. Correspondingly, soul and body are united in one reality. He was the author of the notion of an eternal

Mind which, though itself unmoved, is the Prime Mover of all creation. Some of the current Platonic schools of thought were influenced by Aristotelian ideas, as for example in equating Aristotle's Supreme Mind and Plato's Good. Aristotelian thought, however, did not yet itself constitute a strong contemporary current.

Meantime, Stoicism was winning converts among intellectuals with its strong ethical idealism and personal self-discipline. At the same time it was committed to materialism in the sense that it rejected the Platonic idea of a transcendent world of forms. Its theology could therefore be described as a pantheistic materialism. Spirit is itself material though it infuses and informs matter as the principle of mind or Logos, which was also described as God or Nature. One of the most distinctive ideas of Stoicism was that everything that happens is in response to a divine providence, and man therefore should accept everything with equanimity. The soul of man is an emanation from the Logos, but is not immortal in Plato's sense. Its parts comprise the five senses, the power of articulation, the reproductive capacity, and reason, which is to direct all the others.

We must recognize that both Platonism and Stoicism in this period were influencing each other as well as other philosophies with which they came into contact. Platonism, moreover, had acquired a more theistic emphasis. Meantime, a new system of philosophic thought, known as Neoplatonism arose in the third century under the genius of Plotinus, an Egyptian. God, or the One, is totally transcendent. He is beyond all attributes and above "being" itself. Everything below God is arranged in hierarchical fashion with mind just below God and soul just below mind, which comprises the world of forms. Soul is to be conceived in two parts: the higher, alien to mind, and the lower, or nature, which is soul manifested in the material world.

All individual souls spring from the World-Soul and have a higher element comparable to mind and a lower element represented by the body. Though matter is conceived as evil in Neoplatonism, the world itself is to be thought of as basically good because it has been created by the higher soul; and since all that is can be understood as an "overflow" of the One, as long as men long for reunion with their divine Source, through Eros, all is well. Disciplined purification is necessary so as to release the soul from carnal entanglements. When this is achieved, the cultivation of scientific and philosophic thought becomes possible. Finally, a man may aspire to mystical union with the One, where all distinction is lost, and the eye of the beholder and the eye of the beheld are discovered to be one eye.

The Gnostic World-View

One other important religious current with which Christianity in this period had to come to terms was Gnosticism. The struggle had already begun in apostolic times as reflected in the Fourth Gospel, I John and the Pastoral Epistles. We are not to think here of one entity, which we can carefully define, but as related systems of thought which in their likeness could be described as constituting a distinctive world-view. One should properly think of Gnosticism as a movement rather than a school or institution. It had come into being before Christianity and may even have influenced sects within Judaism. It included in its various forms Jewish, pagan and oriental elements. Gnosticism characteristically combines unbridled speculation with a kind of pseudo-mysticism. There are always graded orders of existence descending in hierarchical fashion from an ineffable Father. The God of the Old Testament is usually downgraded as the creator of the material universe and man. Salvation is brought about through the release of the spiritual element in man, whether this is accomplished by the Father's first-begotten, as in Christian Gnostic circles, or by some other mediator related to Greek or oriental myths.

Gnosticism in all its varied forms was thoroughly dualistic, contrasting the world of spirit and the world of matter, which was thought of as inherently evil. It held that the one true God, the God of light and goodness, could not have created the evil world, which must have come about through some primeval fall or inferior deity. Yet there is also that in man which is of divine origin and longs to return to its source. This requires a mediator or mediators. The mediation takes place through the imparting of secret knowledge. The early church was vulnerable to this movement, as we have seen. It too had, as it were, a secret knowledge, though openly proclaimed ("to know thee, the only true God, and Jesus Christ whom Thou has sent"). Many of the Gnostic teachers sincerely regarded themselves as Christians who were trying to articulate the faith in terms they felt would be more acceptable to their contemporaries. The central issue between developing Christian doctrine and Gnosticism was the ultimate attitude toward the material order and toward history itself. It was in contradistinction to Gnostic ideas in part that the early church shaped its reigning Christology. At the same time, it inadvertently adopted some of the dualism of Gnosticism.

Early Deviations in Doctrine

We have seen how, before the completion of the canon of the New Testament, Jesus had been identified as Lord, and preexistence had been attributed to him. He had been conceived as combining two orders of being, one "according to the flesh," as man, and one "according to the Spirit," as God. Yet he was considered as indivisibly one, at once fully human and fully divine. This basic premise gave rise to all the questions that were to perplex the Church for centuries to come. For our purposes here we should also keep in mind whether the premise in the terms in which it was presented was itself justified from the perspectives with which we shall be considering the Jesus of history and the evolving Christ myth. But for the present, we must follow the historical development.

It is true, we should note in passing, that there was a form of Christology in the second century which denied the divinity altogether. This was known as Ebionism and constituted a sect of Christianity that sought a foothold within Judaism itself. The Ebionites were spiritual descendants of the Judaizers who loom large in the travels of St. Paul; other groups of Christian Jews, such as the Nazaraeans, held to the divinity of Jesus. The Ebionites, for their part, denied a miraculous birth, while retaining the conviction that Jesus was the Messiah and would return to usher in the Davidic kingdom.

Even in non-Jewish circles there was some very early doctrine which denied the presence of the divine element at birth. This has sometimes been called Adoptionism. It conceived that messiahship had been conferred on the man Jesus. It was held that Mary could not have given birth to the Word, but that the Word indwelt Jesus by grace, as indeed he had indwelt Moses and the prophets. The difference was one of degree, not of kind. Jesus was like us in all respects except that the Word, or Holy Spirit, in him was free for unimpeded expression. One cannot resist here the reflection that had this line of thought become the accepted doctrine we should not now be confronted by the necessity of so radical a remythologizing. And one may also ponder the fact that, whereas in physical evolution when a species becomes extinct it cannot later be resuscitated by the arrival of a more favorable environment, with ideas it is otherwise: the form of a myth, rejected initially, may lie fallow for centuries and find resurrection in a new age in the congenial climate afforded by a new world-view.

At the same time, during this early period of wide experimentation in thought, before any creed had become the standard of faith, there was an opposite tendency: it was termed "Docetism." This was the position that since Christ was fully divine he only seemed to suffer and to die. Behind this theological conclusion lay the Gnostic premise that matter is basically evil, even that particular matter which constitutes a man. We have noted traces in the New Testament of reaction against this kind of teaching. In the second century Ignatius condemned those who claimed that Jesus had only appeared to suffer. He held that Docetism was a denial that Jesus had come "according to the flesh," as man. Though the various forms of Gnosticism presented this idea in several ways, the basic contention was that the divine Christ, the Word, had united with the life of the man Jesus at the time of his baptism and indwelt him until the crucifixion. During this period Jesus' body had been transformed into something closer to psychic substance.

Early Apologists for the Faith

While there were these opposing tendencies at either end of the contemporary spectrum of Christian faith, the core of the Church in the liturgy, teaching, and preaching was holding to the New Testament doctrine that the Son of God had in fact become man: Jesus was at once divine and human, spirit and flesh. Defenders of the faith, like Ignatius, asserted: "There is one physician, composed of flesh and of spirit, generate and ingenerate, God in man, authentic life in death, from Mary and from God, first passable and then impassable, Jesus Christ our Lord."

Consensus was that the preexistent Christ-Spirit, the Word, had indwelt the man Jesus of Nazareth. As the apologist Justin Martyr expressed it in the second century, "He who was formerly Logos, and appeared now in the semblance of fire, now in corporeal fashion, has finally by God's will become man for the human race." The incarnation had involved the assumption by Christ the Word, of flesh in Christ Jesus, through miraculous birth. At the same time, the Word remained the Word, the preexistent Christ. If the Logos had found expression in Abraham, Isaac, and Moses, why should he not indwell the man Jesus? Justin Martyr seems to have believed that the Word is in fact present in all men in some degree, in much the same way that Quakers later asserted that there was that of God in all men. He even speaks of the Word as present in man like a seed. Some have thought that for Justin Martyr the Word, or Logos, substituted in Jesus for what in other men the contemporary Stoics had called the human rational soul. In any case he seems to have been influenced by Stoic thought in considering the Word as "the governing principle" in Jesus the man. Though the Word is present in all men in part, he is fully present in Jesus. Once again, had this line of thought become the orthodox strain, perhaps we should not now find it necessary to engage in such radical remythologizing.

Early Western Speculation on the Two Natures

Sometimes, as in Irenaeus, we see how a man's Christology is given its shape in the process of articulating opposition to contemporaries believed to be heretics. Hence, in condemning current forms of Gnosticism and Docetism, Irenaeus stresses the unity of the God-man. He insists that only if the Divine Word became fully human could our redemption be accomplished. Irenaeus saw Jesus as the second Adam, sanctifying the entire race of man from Adam forward by virtue of having assumed human flesh.

One of the great theologians in the West, at the close of

the second century and the beginning of the third, was
the North African, Tertullian. He stressed the presence in
Jesus of two substances and was among the first to reflect
upon the relationship of these two substances. He asks,
was the Word "metamorphosed" into flesh at Jesus' birth,
or did he "clothe" himself in it, and replies firmly that the
former could not have been the case since the Word, like
God himself, is immutable. Both substances, the divine
and the human, remain unchanged in the union. Here he
clearly anticipates later developments, crystallized ultimately in the creeds. The divine is responsible for the
miracles, the human is heir to the suffering common to all
men. Yet while spirit and flesh remain distinct they are
present in one person, Jesus. "We observe a twofold condition, not confused but conjoined, Jesus in one Person at
once God and man." If Tertullian embraced paradox, in
the end he defended his position with the famous dictum,
"*Certum est quia impossible*" or "I believe it because it is
absurd."

Imaginative and Mystical Speculation in the East

Though it may be said that in Tertullian the West
achieved a mature Christology earlier than the East, we
must turn to the East for the interplay of imaginative
speculation and ascetic experimentation. Sharing Tertullian's view as far as the fact of the incarnation was concerned, Origen of Alexandria in the first half of the third
century expressed the traditional belief in picturesque
language: "We believe that the very Logos of the Father,
the Wisdom of God Himself, was enclosed within the limits of that man who appeared in Judaea; nay more, that
God's wisdom entered a woman's womb, was born as an
infant, and wailed like crying children."

But, in answer to the question as to how the divine and
human were related in Jesus, Origen made quite a different
reply. Origen believed in the preexistence of *all* souls, not

that of Jesus alone. The soul of Jesus was in all respects like the souls of other men, save that it had become attached to the Word in mystical devotion, whereas all other souls had fallen away. Hence, when this particular soul was born as Jesus, Godhead and manhood were united. While Origen recognizes the two natures, both of which retained their identity, the divine nature, the nature of the Word, has the ascendancy. This duality is so profound that the divine nature does not undergo any of the experiences of either the body or soul. Yet Jesus is conceived as one man, retaining an interior unity. He is a "composite" entity. The unity is more than a combination; it is a "commingling" which affects the deification of the human. Hence the unity of the Word and the humanity in Jesus is more complete than had been attained in the prophets. Jesus' human soul was thoroughly suffused with the Word, which in turn became the "governing principle" of his life. There remains a touch of the Gnostic in Origen at the point where he suggests that Jesus was able to alter his body, whenever he willed to do so, into an ethereal substance. At the time of the resurrection the union between the Word and the transformed body became final and the two natures indistinguishable.

It will be apparent that in his concept of the preexistence of all souls, Origin introduced an idea that was not destined to be retained in evolving Christian doctrine. With its rejection so also Origen's notion of how the divine and human were related was also necessarily abandoned. Origen's immediate successors held that the humanity of Jesus did not include a human soul at all, the Word assuming the function normally allocated to the soul. In the last half of the third century it was said by one theologian that the divine Logos was in Jesus what the interior man (or soul) is in other men.

The Arian Heresy

While the christological debate continued, the myth of the Trinity was concurrently developing. At the time of the Church's first great ecumenical council, the Council of Nicaea in 325, the focus of attention was on the interrelationship of God the Father, God the Son and God the Holy Spirit. The first credal statement bearing the authorization of the whole Church was concerned to assert the humanity of Jesus as against Gnostic tendencies, on the one hand, and to proclaim his lordship as against Arian tendencies, on the other. The Church had already ruled on Docetism and Gnosticism, in one sense, through established tradition. Now it officially spoke out against the leader of the new heresy, Arius, who did not, in the judgment of the Church, sufficiently accept the divinity of Jesus. The Arians held to the transcendence of the one God. Even the Word was for them a created being, not co-eternal with the Father. They insisted that the Son had a beginning even as the Word had a beginning, whereas God had no beginning. They tirelessly repeated the claim with reference to the Son: "There was when He was not." Even though the Son is God's Word and Wisdom, he is to be considered separate from that Word and that Wisdom which are part of the essence of God because he too is a creature. Arius put it this way: "The Father remains ineffable to the Son, and the Word can neither see nor know the Father perfectly and accurately . . . but what He knows and sees, He knows and sees proportionately to His capacity, just as our knowledge is adapted to our powers."

The inference is that the Son must therefore be capable even of sin. To make this deviant view more palatable Arius safeguarded by suggesting that nevertheless God had taken care lest Jesus sin by providing for him abundant grace. Arius even went so far as to say of the Son,

"Even if He is called God, He is not God truly, but by participation in grace." Meantime, Arius and his followers thought of themselves not as originators of these ideas but as carrying on one strand of tradition established by Origen and Dionysius of Alexandria. And they also turned to copious scriptural texts for supplemental confirmation. Philosophically some of their assumptions were more akin to Aristotle than Plato, and they did not share the Neoplatonic view that the same reality can exist at different levels.

At the Council of Nicaea, called in 325 by Constantine, the teaching of Arius was condemned and even his colleague and supporter, Eusebius of Caesarea, was provisionally excommunicated. The creed which became the instrument of the council, binding on the Church, asserted clearly that the Son is "begotten, not made." The irony is that, while the intention of Arius was simply to safeguard the unity of the Godhead, his victorious opponent, Athanasius, also charged him with making the liturgical practice of baptizing in the name of the Trinity null and void, and of subverting the salvational doctrine that redemption was possible through the presence in Christ of both natures.

The key word in the historic decision for Athanasius and opposed to Arius was the Greek word *homoousios*, meaning "of one substance." Whether this was intended at the time to be understood in a generic sense, "of the same nature," or in the sense of numerical identity, scholars disagree. In any case it was intended to establish beyond the shadow of a doubt that the Son was fully God by insisting that he shared the same divine nature with the Father. Both Athanasius and Arius would have agreed to all intents and purposes on the unity of the Godhead. The issue was whether the Son and the Holy Spirit were co-eternal with the Father or whether "there was when they were not."

Unless we are to take the view that when the Church spoke in ecumenical council, before the major divisions took place, it spoke infallibly for all time, we may once again ponder which position entertained by different groups in the Church at this juncture is actually more compatible with our contemporary world-view, shaped as it is by our recently acquired perspectives of evolution and depth psychology. Some of us would be inclined to raise questions in addition about the validity of a decision influenced by the reigning emperor, Constantine, who was obviously not a trained theologian.

In any case, the decision made was by no means instantly accepted. There arose a considerable anti-Nicene protest which even carried the day for a time in successive synods at Sirmium (357), Nicé (359), and Constantinople (360). Not until the Council of Constantinople in 381 was the Arian position finally crushed. Even numerical identity as distinct from generic was now established. As Athanasius put it, "He [the Son] is the offspring of His Father's substance, so that no man may doubt that in virtue of His likeness to His immutable Father the Word is also immutable." Still more unequivocally: "the divinity of the Father is identical with that of the Son"; even "The Son's divinity is the Father's divinity." The final word, in a sense, is that the divine *ousia*, or substance, is indivisible, at once Father and Son. The die was cast. Henceforth, orthodoxy was to insist that the difference between Jesus and other men was one of kind, not of degree. Jesus alone was divine, of one substance with God.

Continued Speculation on the Relation between the Two Natures

But the Nicene decision, confirmed and clarified by the Council of Constantinople in 381, left unresolved the relationship between the two natures in Jesus himself. This had become the inherent christological problem as the result of the decision that Jesus was fully divine. How could Jesus be at once fully God *and* fully man? There were two basic views abroad. The Arian one was that in Jesus the Word had united himself to a human body without the presence of a rational soul whose place he took. This made possible the idea of a unity in Jesus of the two natures based on the notion that Jesus was made flesh but not man because he did not have a human soul. He was therefore not complete man. There is a curious irony here in that, on the one hand, the Arian doctrine denied full divinity and, on the other, it called into question full humanity. The other basic view came to be called the Antiochene position and was articulated by Eustathius of Antioch. This strain of thought insisted that Jesus had both a human soul and a human body, but also asserted that the human soul had been deified by its association with the Word. Some have distinguished these two contending views as representing Word-flesh (Alexandrian) and Word-man (Antiochene) types of Christology. Both were attempting to come to terms with the prevailing philosophical and psychological concepts of the contemporary world-view.

We shall not undertake to pursue the argument that continued for nearly another century. Suffice it to say that Pope Leo issued in 449 the celebrated Tome which declared the unity of the person of the God-man with that of the divine Word. It affirmed the coexistence of the two natures in the one person without mixture or confusion. Though these two natures operate in harmony, they operate separately. Finally, they combine in the sense that we can say the Son of God was crucified and buried and that the Son of Man came down from heaven. This was as close as the Church had come to meeting the demands of both sides.

The Council of Chalcedon in 451, with more than five hundred bishops present, canonized Leo's Tome and produced a new formal confession of faith, reaffirming the two natures without confusion in the one person. It deliberately undertook to give equal recognition to the unity and to the duality of the God-man. The two natures retain their distinctive qualities and operations within the union.

The first great creative period of theological debate on Christology was at an end. The early church fathers had added the weight of their deliberations and their prestige to the authority of the Scriptures. Decisions made by the ecumenical councils of the first five centuries were to be cited along with Scriptures henceforth, by orthodox groups, as the basis of authority in matters of doctrine, especially Christology. The tolerances had been set within which judgment could be pronounced as to whether any new variant was orthodox or heretical. But it must be remembered that the intellectual environment in which the concepts had been hammered out was shaped by the prevailing philosophy and psychology of the ancient world. When substantial changes in these disciplines of thought were later to emerge, constituting radically new and different world-views, christological concepts would have to change if they were to be assimilated by those who embraced these new world-views with religious passion to keep their world one.

II. Rational Empiricism and the Death of the Christ Myth

The Long Interlude before the Age of Enlightenment

Throughout the Middle Ages the process of theological speculation remained deductive. This is to say that theologians began with the unexamined premises of doctrine in the Scriptures, now supplemented by the creeds of the ecumenical councils and papal decrees, and proceeded to defend these on the basis of the principles of logic, making use of the method of dialectics. It was not yet a question of asking the fundamental question: How is truth known in the sphere of religion? The truth had been made known once and for all through specific, biblical revelation. It was a question only of proving the cogency of revealed truth and of systematizing the ramifications.

The result was the creation of a world-view of great inclusiveness, known as Scholasticism. Within this world-view it was taken for granted that theology was the queen of the sciences and the master of the arts. Platonic "realism," in which eternal forms possessed objective reality, was superseded by the limited realism of Aristotle. It is true that Anselm produced in the eleventh century a new theory of the atonement, abrogating the traditional metaphor of a ransom paid the devil in favor of the metaphor of satisfaction due the offended moral judgment of God. But despite the progidious intellectual achievement, one might say the rational tour-de-force, of the theology of Thomas Aquinas, there was no other significant change in the christology of the Church. No secular world-view had been put together of sufficient independence and integrity to demand a new Christology.

When the Reformation came, at length, it was not the Christology of the Church that was challenged, but rather the elaborate system of merit accumulation through Mary and the saints (in addition to that of Jesus) that could be drawn upon in the form of indulgences. The point of contention was the method of salvation. Piecemeal repentance, related to indulgences, was rejected. The whole life of the penitent must be involved. Good works availed nothing. They will follow faith as the fruit of obedience; but salvation is by the grace of faith. Yet the Christology of Luther was basically conservative. He confirmed the ecumenical creeds and enthusiastically commended the Chalcedonian summary of the two natures of Christ. It is true that he developed a concept he referred to as the organic union between the divine and the human Jesus, accomplished through the incarnation of the Logos. Relying upon the grace of God in Christ, and this *by faith alone*, he did achieve a limited Pauline mysticism. But we cannot attribute to him a significant contribution toward the development of the Christ myth. The same must be said of John Calvin.

It was not until a substantially new world-view had been shaped, in large part by the philosophical inquiry of Descartes and Spinoza in the eighteenth century, that radical change was demanded in the traditional Christ myth. In theological thought this meant successively the rise of deism in England, naturalism in France, and rationalism in Germany. Orthodoxy, whether Roman Catholic, Lutheran, Calvinistic, or Anglican, generally speaking has continued to hold fast to the Christ myth in its primitive form, but at the expense of a deeply divided world-view which applies deductive reasoning in one area of human experience and inductive in another. The religious instinct "to get it all together" is held in abeyance with tortured and specious reasoning. It remains to comment on two historical developments which were committed to getting it all together: the empiricism of rationalism which ultimately abandoned the Christ myth in its attempt to keep the world one; and the empiricism of mysticism which kept the world one by permitting the myth to evolve.

Deism in England

It was the objective of the deists to uncover and to explore a "natural religion" which would draw all men and obviate distasteful theological dispute. Moral concern was part of the motivation, and the deists set about discovering the moral imperative inherent in natural reli-

gion. The name "Deism" was chosen in deliberate coun-
terdistinction to atheism. God was the "first cause" who
had set in motion unchanging laws which accounted for
sequences of cause and effect.

The modern age of scientific investigation had dawned,
with Francis Bacon, as early as the late sixteenth century.
The great shift in the method of inquiry, from the deductive process, applied by theology to the revelation of
Scripture, to the inductive method, had been established
in the natural sciences. In philosophy, in psychology, and
in theology the new approach would come to be called
"the empirical method" in the quest for truth. It was
destined to have far-reaching reverberations in all these
disciplines of human inquiry. It would give rise ultimately
to the philosophy of religion, reversing the historical
ascendency of the Middle Ages in the relationship between philosophy and theology. The method of Scholasticism, for those who were constrained to assimilate theology into a world-view dominated by the new science
and philosophy, had been discredited once and for all. It
was no longer possible to deduce doctrinal positions from
so-called historical revelation; for the deists it was possible to arrive at such positions only by induction from
present experience. Natural theology was to become almost a branch of philosophy, which had usurped the
throne and once more become, as in ancient Greece,
queen of the sciences and master of the arts.

The influence of Spinoza on the English deists was even
greater than that of Bacon. He held that the miraculous
element in religion must be dispensed with. The supernatural, as distinct from the natural, must be abandoned.
Spinoza's thought was close to pantheism; certainly it was
an intellectual monism of a mystical type.

With Thomas Hobbes in the seventeenth century,
psychology was freed from dependence on theology, as
philosophy had already been released from this bondage.

Ethics was to be derived not from theology but from a new psychology, supported by civil and social considerations. Writing during this period dominated politically by Cromwell, Hobbes defended the right of the State to intervene in spiritual affairs on the basis of his social philosophy in the *Leviathan*. He defended absolute monarchy as opposed to the democratic tendencies that were astir in the contemporary spiritualist movements.

It will be recollected how dependent theological developments of the early church were upon the prevailing psychological concepts of Plato and the Aristotelian and Stoic variations. If inherited orthodox theological doctrines were in part established on assumptions about the nature of the human psyche, it is not surprising that when a new philosophy made credible new and different psychological assumptions, a shaking of theological foundations inevitably ensued. Hobbes, in his psychological speculation, had arrived at two radically new assertions about man: "All that exists is body" and "all that occurs is motion." There is no preexistent soul, no rational principle as distinct from the body. Knowledge does not spring from intuitive recognition of universal forms; it derives from impressions on the brain made mechanically through nerve senses stimulated by external objects.

In reaching this conclusion Hobbes had been influenced by Kepler, Galileo and the French scientists. It has been said of psychology, in a citation at the conferring of a graduate degree, that it is "the oldest of the arts, the newest of the sciences." If psychology had heretofore been more of an art, as well as a field of philosophical speculation, it became now, at least in aspiration, a science. Hobbes simply extended the mechanical conception of the physical world to the description of the processes of the mind.

The deists were applying this new mechanistic worldview to theological speculation. They held that subjective reason is the principle of religious truth. They agreed with Locke that the truths which purportedly came through divine revelation were acceptable only if they were compatible with a reasonable metaphysics and met the test of natural ethics. The final test was perception through experience. In Locke's view the Christian religion was not in its essentials in conflict with natural religion but must submit at all points to the established criteria of natural and universal religion, and be reasonable. The conservatives, on the other hand, were insisting that, whereas natural religion existed, the dominant characteristic of Christianity is its supernatural element.

David Hume carried still further some of the directions assumed by the new emphasis on empiricism. If experience is the sole foundation of knowledge, we must be skeptical of the existence of both substance and causality. Substance has never been perceived in a strict sense; nor has causality. Indeed, all matter, as far as can be ascertained, may be only a figment of the imagination. Only those deductions which can be demonstrated mathematically can be trusted; hence most claims of causality are suspect. What we normally call the mind is only a collection of impressions, not a distinct reality or substance. Thus Hume proposed to carry skepticism even further than Berkeley, who had denied reality only to matter. Hume would extend the doubt to embrace mind and soul. The very roots of religious experience were thereby called into question. The argument had come full circle. If the concept of cause and effect were done away, deism's central tenet was done away. The deistic proofs of the existence of God, the teleological, cosmological, and moral, could no longer stand.

Naturalism in France

The counterpart in France of the deists in England was

the naturalists. The movement was known as the Enlightenment. There was no counterpart of free-thinkers among the theologians, however. Therefore, the movement was largely a secular one. Voltaire himself became a deist under the influence of a visit to England, 1726–29. Like other deists, he opposed revealed religion and rejected authority based on the Bible and tradition. He ridiculed with his merciless wit the spirit of dogmatism and its periodic indulgence in persecution. What he valued in Christianity was the Platonic strain which made it, for him, "respectable." Voltaire's colleagues, Helvetius, de La Mettrie and Diderot, carried the naturalism progressively into atheistic materialism. Jean Jacques Rousseau turned the naturalism of the day into a philosophy advocating return to nature, a naïve acceptance of the goodness of nature coupled with the conviction that only man is vile. Man had been good as long as he remained close to nature and until he was corrupted by civilization. A return to nature would heal him and enable him to recover his pristine purity. The French free-thinkers laid the intellectual framework for the articulation of the ideas behind the French Revolution, an event which, in itself, could only be viewed, from any perspective, as a mixed blessing.

Rationalism in Germany

Though the new rationalism was slower in making headway in Germany, the home of the Reformation where confessionalism generally still held sway, after it did arrive in force it made perhaps still more notable impact on subsequent theological development.

One of the early advocates, Leibnitz, attempted to reconcile natural religion and supernatural revelation. He was a profound optimist and believed that the existence of a God, at once all-powerful and good, could be demonstrated by logical proof. Later, in his *Critique of Pure*

Reason, Immanuel Kant challenged such optimism. On the other hand, in his *Critique of Practical Reason* Kant allowed for rationalism a role in the discovery and advocacy of the moral imperative. In *Religion within the Limits of Pure Reason* he attempted a defense of natural religion on ethical grounds which has laid the foundation for much of "modernist" theology ever since. J. F. Roehr stood in this succession. It is interesting to see the effect the rationalist world-view was having on the Christ myth. Said Roehr: "Jesus was a man like ourselves in the fullest and in a comprehensive meaning of that term, a natural product of his people and his age, but in regard to spirit, wisdom, virtue and religion excelled by no mortal of the past or future, a hero of humanity in the highest sense."

The Impact of Philosophical Empiricism on Theology

The demands of the new philosophical empiricism had their inevitable effect on the Christ myth within the religious communities that accepted this approach to knowledge as applicable even within the sphere of theology. Partly, the philosophical reevaluation was stimulated by the excesses of the confessionalism of the preceding age. The principle of interpenetration and interaction, observed in the science of ecology in our time, with reference to the biosphere, applies as well within a given segment of the noosphere. There was a reaction against the concept of the total depravity of man, producing a new humanism that took an encouraging view of the nature of man, a view that would have been condemned at an earlier time as the heresy of Pelagianism. But now that the Church was no longer one, anathema could no longer effectively be pronounced on free-thinkers who ran afoul of orthodoxy. There was no longer one hierarchy that held the keys to the kingdom.

It might be said that the rationalist theologians of the three types considered remained Jesus-centered, but were no longer Christ-centered. Jesus was the ideal man, no longer the God-man. This position harks back to the Ebionitism of the early Jewish sect within Christianity and looks to the later Socinianism but goes further to the left than either group. It is as if the spectrum were widening at either end. Others to the right were losing their grasp on the human element. Meantime, the rationalists had made significant contributions to the whole Church, including historical studies of Bible texts and of doctrinal developments, and had initiated a new study, the philosophy of religion.

One stream of the rationalist theologians had become Socinians, the forerunners of the Unitarians. The earliest ingredients were the rationalism of Duns Scotus and the humanism of the kind espoused by Erasmus. The early Socinians retained the authority of Scriptures and gave place to a supernatural element as long as both passed the canons of the reasonable. Their emphasis was on the unity of God and the free will of man. Though more wise and much more pure than other men, Jesus was yet a man. He was neither preexistent nor in the traditional sense the Logos incarnate. He was not the only Son of God, but among all the sons of God he was preeminent. The Socinians rejected also the traditional theories of the atonement. Man's guilt for sin cannot be transferred to another. But Jesus is still our Saviour by virtue of the example of his moral character and his assurance of our forgiveness by God through repentance and obedience. After 1860 the Socinians on the Continent were in communication formally with the Unitarians in England and America.

Generally speaking, though there were exceptions, Unitarianism was moving to the left of the Socinians. In point of fact, in Unitarianism one can see that the Christ myth no longer exists as a myth. Jesus as a man may remain central in the interest of some Unitarians within the context of the eclectic process of drawing material from other religions. But Unitarianism has cut itself off from its roots and has become increasingly an ethical-culture society. One might say that within this milieu the myth had died rather than continued to evolve in a viable form.

The same might be said of that strand of development which stemmed from the revival of philosophical idealism of the Renaissance and of Humanism in Germany through Kant, Lessing, Schiller, Goethe, and Hegel. Kant had made reason the criterion of sound religion. One's first responsibility was to listen to the voice of conscience, the moral imperative. While there is no ontological proof of the existence of God, there is proof through the *experienced* moral consciousness of man. The will of man is free to become obedient to conscience. The struggle between good and evil does go on in man, but response in faith to the moral character of Jesus can provide motivation to the will. He rejected the supernatural and the miraculous in Scripture and believed that passages must be sifted for relevance on the basis of reasonableness.

The classic period of German literature was related to the philosophical idealism which Kant had introduced. It flourished in the last half of the eighteenth and first half of the nineteenth centuries. Meantime, Lessing, Schiller, and Goethe still further idealized the thought of Kant. Finding the evangelical position of the confessional churches distasteful, these literary artists were in effect, however unconsciously, attempting to inaugurate a new religion which would combine elements from ancient classicism, the new humanism, mysticism, and a love of nature. But they were unable to establish an unbroken continuity with the central ideas of historical Christianity, since they had unwittingly severed the tap root of Biblicism and had not discovered a way to allow the Christ myth to continue to live by continuing to evolve.

III.   Mystical Empiricism and the Evolving Christ Myth

The Empiricism of Mystical Experience

But there was one strand of continuity within Christendom which permitted the Christ myth to continue to evolve in an organic way. This was what we have called the apostolic succession of the mystics. They were able to provide the milieu in which the myth could survive, and flourish as it evolved, because their ultimate source of authority was neither revelation in Scripture, nor hierarchical decree, but first-hand religious experience, interpreted by reason. In effect they were already committed to a form of empiricism: reflection upon present experience, further tested by experimentation. Instead of beginning from unexamined premises of biblical revelation and ecumenical proclamation, and deducing therefrom a philosophical or theological system, they characteristically engaged in inductive reasoning from existential experience, verifiable by the peculiar experimentation of obedience.

The mystics do not confuse symbols with reality, because they have been vouchsafed direct experience of ultimate reality. Therefore they instinctively recognize that doctrines are to be understood as metaphors whose validity is always to be further tested in experimentation, never as dogmas to be embraced as literally true. They are therefore free to allow all metaphors, including the Christ myth, to continue to evolve.

E. Herman opens her fine study entitled *The Meaning and Value of Mysticism* with the observation:

Beneath the currents which by action and reaction have gone to shape Christian thought there sounds, like the fabled sunken bell, the strain of Mysticism. Thrust down by victorious institutional, rational and moralistic forces, the mystic note floats up from the depths—now muffled, now clear. Every now and

again the penalty of success overtakes the ruling system, and
Christian men, disillusioned by a hollow civilization and an
externalized Church, listen to the submerged melody and find
it a song of deliverance; and out of such moments of reaction
are born the great spiritual movements, whether explicitly
mystical or only showing deep affinities with Mysticism.[1]

We have seen how the two great mystics of the Apostolic Church, Paul and the author of the Fourth Gospel,
were both able to make major contributions to the evolving Christ myth out of their own first-hand religious
experience. From his personal experience on the road to
Damascus, which had involved for him an existential
death and resurrection, Paul was able to shape a new
facet to the evolving Christ myth: the metaphor of dying
to sin and rising to newness of life, in which the experienced presence of the indwelling Christ permitted one to
enter the kingdom now. Whether the author of the Fourth
Gospel was the apostle John or another, a miraculous personal transformation had taken place through direct mystical experience of unity with God through Christ. Reflection upon the meaning of the mystical experience
produced the great prelude on the Logos and led to an
emphasis on the Eucharist as a recurring symbol of sustained being-in-God through identification of the Logos or
Holy Spirit in us with the Logos in Jesus.

Though the mystical strain is perceptible in some of the
ideas of Origen and of others of the early church fathers,
the next great figure of the succession might be said to be
Augustine. His mysticism was of the "being-in-God" variety, like that of the Fourth Gospel, as distinct from the
"being-in-Christ" of Paul. But the experience was understood as organically related to the Christ myth. Augustine

[1] E. Herman, *The Meaning and Value of Mysticism* (London: James
Clarke and Co., 1915), p. 3.

saw himself as condemned to restlessness until he found his rest in God. While he was prepared to relate his very creative thinking to the Bible and the decisions of the ecumenical councils, his private source of ultimate authority was his own mystical experience. One cannot but wistfully reflect on what it might have meant in terms of subsequent development within the Church had his mystical approach to religious experience prevailed over the rational approach advocated by Scholasticism.

The Rise of Monastic Mysticism

Mysticism, which had advocates within the Church from the beginning, as we have seen, responding to the mysticism in Jesus himself, now began to flourish again, this time fused with the ascetic ideals of monasticism. Its first advocate of stature during this period was John Duns Scotus. An original thinker and philosopher, he constructed a bridge from Neoplatonism to the speculative mysticism of the Middle Ages. He translated the writings of Dionysius the Areopagite into Latin. The new piety took the form of a passionate desire to follow Jesus vicariously and, insofar as possible, practically, in the stages of his human suffering. The object was to become like the Saviour himself through the imitation of his earthly life.

If John Duns Scotus had charted this mystic path intellectually, though not characteristically a mystic himself, the first dedicated adventurer on the way was Hugo, preceptor of the Abbey School of St. Victor in the environs of Paris in the latter part of the twelfth century. The motivation seems not unlike the Pauline passion to win salvation through interior union with Jesus the Christ. It was Bernard of Clairvaux, however, who gave classic expression to this rediscovered Christ mysticism. This mystic way began to be defined in terms of the disciplined life and the successive stages of attainment.

The sequence begins with meditation on the holiness and purity of the man Jesus, which produces a profound conviction of one's own sinfulness and the fear of the impending wrath of God. This leads to abandoning one's self to the mercy of Jesus, which in turn assures forgiveness by God, after penitence. The second movement is the willed and disciplined imitation of the love, patience, humility and obedience of the earthly Jesus. The objective is the surrender of one's own will to the will of God through the imitation of Jesus, which has been variously known as proficiency or illumination. The third movement is the unwilled ecstasy of union.

It will be seen that, though this was not a fresh contribution to Christology in terms of doctrine, it was a new witness to the humanity of the historical Jesus. The new piety undertook to identify with Jesus' suffering and obedience as a man. The ecstatic union, moreover, was not sought for its own sake. To become, in Augustine's sense, to the Almighty as a man's right arm is to a man, an instrument in the service of God, was the motivation. If the ecstatic union was granted in addition, this was a grace that could in no way be merited.

Some men are seminal thinkers. They plant the seeds of thought in the minds of others which in turn generate new patterns of thought. Others, like Bernard of Clairvaux, could be said to be seminal doers. Their actions set in motion a chain of reactions which motivate others to similar acts of dedication through moral effort. Bernard stands at the fountainhead of the monastic movement which has proliferated through the centuries and is still very much alive seven centuries later. Likewise, Francis of Assisi, who embraced Lady Poverty and carried the imitation of Jesus to new heights of intensity, still speaks to our condition. The mystic way, based as it is upon experience and the cultivation of an innate faculty in man continues to make its claims in the modern world even when it is described in new language, appropriate to changing world-views.

The Flowering of Mysticism in the Fourteenth Century

In England, Duns Scotus at the close of the thirteenth century had begun to challenge the supremacy of Scholastic thought as represented by Thomas Aquinas. He confronted the Aristotelian approach with a revival of Augustinianism and the Platonic. He criticized the emphasis on intellectual speculation and attempted to make theological inquiry more of a practical science. He saw God in more personal terms, as exacting response of will rather than intellect. Scholasticism had tended to put God in a box constructed of intellectual ideas. Duns Scotus was impelled to recover for God the dimension of otherness and unpredictable freedom. In Scholastic terms God theoretically must will the preconceived good; for Duns Scotus whatever God wills *is* the good. A difference of perspective perhaps, but one that has far-reaching implications.

Meantime, the new piety which had emerged in the mystical strain of monasticism in the eleventh and twelfth centuries had begun to bear more fruit. Though theology in the monasteries had become officially Thomistic, it had been infused with Platonic and Neoplatonic principles which had filtered into the West through the writings of the Areopagite and John Scotus Erigena. By the fifteenth century, lay movements like the Brothers of the Common Life had been quickened by the influence of monastic mysticism. But the fourteenth century has been identified as the time of the flowering of mysticism. Major mystics like Meister Eckhart, Henry Suso, John Tauler, and John Ruysbroeck had arisen. The rationalists and the ecclesiastics among the theologians have always looked askance at mysticism, suspicious, not without some justification, that the free spirit of the mystic, with his independent and

immanent source of authority in direct experience, constituted a threat both to theological conformity and ecclesi-
astic discipline. It was not surprising that Meister Eckhart
was pronounced a heretic after his death.

Nevertheless some have recognized that the real seeds
of the Reformation lay in the certainty and courage imparted by the mystical experience of a man like Meister
Eckhart. And it is significant that the mystical faculty in
Martin Luther was awakened by the anonymous *Theo-
logia Germanica* which he pondered and was led to edit
and to reedit. In England as well as on the Continent,
mysticism was flourishing in the fourteenth century.
Richard Rolle, Walter Hilton, and Julian of Norwich, as
well as the anonymous Cloud of Unknowing, were interpreting the mystical experience. In the expanding response, deep spoke unto deep.

As the Middle Ages drew to a close, what may be called
a theology of merit, or good works, dominated. But the
mystics and the humanists had made their respective witness in such a way as to produce a shaking of the foundations for those perceptive enough to recognize what was
happening. Both had implanted depth charges which
were presently to explode, creating a great divide from
which much of Christendom could never again return to
the comfortable security of the Scholastic world-view.

In the sixteenth century, Teresa of Ávila and John of
the Cross gave classic expression to the mystical experience. They were reticent about the authenticity of the
psychic phenomena with which the vision was sometimes
associated. But they never doubted the experience of
union with God. Their faith rested ultimately on this empirical authority.

*New Currents of Mystical Experience after the Refor-
mation*

As the stream of continuity comprising the advocates of

reason as the ultimate source of authority, whether consciously so designated or not, and having its fountainhead in the rationalism of ancient Greece, found its contemporary forms of renewal in the seventeenth century, so another ancient, yet ever recurring spring of independent exploration was being tapped by other leaders in Christendom: first-hand mystical experience. As the ultimate source of authority, the mystics and their followers turned primarily neither to Scriptures, nor to the Fathers, nor to the Councils, but to interior guidance by the Spirit, or the Inner Light. They too could trace their heritage to roots more ancient than the canonized Scriptures themselves. These men held that the Word resided in man before it permeated the Scriptures, and only the Word in man was qualified to interpret the Word in Scripture.

The new form assumed by this movement was designated "spiritualism." It recognized its own apostolic succession: Plato, Neoplatonism, Origen, Pseudo-Dionysius, Augustine, Scotus Erigena, Bernard of Clairvaux. Some of the contemporaries of Luther had stood in this stream of influence, notably A. B. Karlstadt, Kaspar Schwenkfeld, and Sebastian Franck. One of the greatest in the seventeenth century was Jacob Boehme. Mystics generally have always insisted on the distinction between symbols and the realities to which they point. The more perceptive among them have always recognized that doctrines or dogmas represent theological reflection in the shape of metaphors on some aspect of the experience of the living God. To fix or to impale God on the thorn of such metaphors is as much idolatry as to fashion graven images purporting to be physical likenesses of him. We are not to understand the atonement as some kind of binding transaction to appease an angry God, but as an "at-one-ment" in proportion as the life of Jesus draws us irresistibly to plant our feet on the "royal way of the holy cross." Angelus Selisius, in the seventeenth century, set this approach to the music of poetry:

> Though Christ a thousand times
> In Bethlehem be born,
> If He's not born in Thee
> Thy soul is still forlorn. . . .
> The cross on Golgotha
> Will never save thy soul
> The cross in thine own heart
> Alone can make thee whole.

Similarly, formal baptism is considered symbolic of the true inward baptism into the Spirit that was in Jesus. The bread and wine in the Eucharist represent the same Spirit that is to be inwardly received and assimilated.

The counterpart in England to the Anabaptist movement on the Continent was a group known as the Familists which came from Holland, the "Seekers" and the Quakers. There was in these groups not only a reaction against church forms but also against rigidity in theological statement. Revelation was not limited to the Scriptures, though members of these groups had profound respect for the Scriptures and were thoroughly familiar with their contents. The authority to be trusted was the light within. The emphasis in Christology was not on the extrinsic benefits wrought by Christ on the cross, but the intrinsic benefits realized through consciousness of the Christ within. It is the ever present Christ in the heart of the believer who ministers to his own, even now.

Perhaps the most distinctive characteristic of the leaders of the Society of Friends, George Fox, William Penn, and Robert Barclay, was the peculiar balance in them between cultivation of the inward life, the "life that is hid with Christ in God" as Paul expressed it, and passion for social reform. It was an activist mysticism or mystical activism. And for the first time there was a deliberate cultivation of the corporate dimension of the mystical experience in the meeting for worship. In the ministry of the Word, it was Christ himself who spoke.

Schleiermacher belongs in this succession of mystics. Though he descended from a family of Reformed preachers and was influenced early by the Moravians, he was an independent thinker of original genius. He could not accept the confessional interpretation of the atonement, and rejected the concept of eternal punishment. Yet he retained a Christ-centered emphasis. An eclectic spirit, he drew on Aristotle, Plato, Spinoza, and the Romantics. He wanted to harmonize culture and religion, creating a synthesis between the spirit of the new science and the ancient theology.

His was a subjective theology of feeling. He identified the most characteristic religious feeling as that of dependency upon God, the feeling of the creature for the Creator. The marks of the spirit of true religion for Schleiermacher were reverence, humility, gratitude, joy, confidence, trust. His own religion was a form of mysticism approaching pantheism. Revelation is unfinished and may take infinite form in present intuitions of the nature of the universe. He wanted to rewed philosophy and theology, but on a basis in which there would be a reversal of dominancy within the union. Theology would be replaced by a philosophy of religion. Salvation takes place not by the efficacy of an exterior atonement but by a kind of mystical fellowship with Christ in which deep-going moral conversion is accomplished. If his theological position was, on the one hand, a kind of philosophy of religion, it was, on the other hand, a kind of modern psychology of religion. If he was an intellectual genius, he was also a prophet, anticipating much that was to follow in both the liberal and the conservative camps.

Samuel Taylor Coleridge was the first in the succession of liberal theologians in England. He had an integrative

mind and was a seminal thinker, in some respects a kind
of British equivalent of Schleiermacher. He was a man of
parts, bringing a great deal together in his focus upon any
issue. He had the quality of universalism in the breadth of
his outlook. A Romantic by nature, he opposed the materialism abroad in philosophy. But on the other hand he
objected to the dogmatic position of the Evangelicals. He
believed religion to be part of the native endowment of
man, along with innate ethical judgment and free will. On
the matter of authority he looked basically to subjective
experience, as have all the mystics, for indeed he was one.
While distinguishing between reason and understanding,
he held that nothing may be accepted as creed which
cannot be defended by reason. While he turned to the
Bible for personal inspiration by the Word, he felt no
inconsistency in subjecting the Scriptures to critical
study. True reason and right faith can never be opposed,
in the nature of the case. One may place him also among
the earliest of the conscious advocates of that form of empiricism embraced by mystics.

Mysticism in the Twentieth Century

In his widely influential book, *The Idea of the Holy*,
Rudolph Otto allows in human experience for the existence of the super-rational as well as the rational. The
"holy" is the word symbol for the numinous element
which provokes awe and wonder and irresistibly attracts as
well as judges. Albert Schweitzer's equivalent for the idea
of the holy in human experience was "reverence for life,"
again an existential reality arising out of the depths of
mystical experience and itself constituting a moral imperative for ethical action. Both Otto and Schweitzer,
each in his own distinctive way, were bearing witness to
the mystical approach to religious experience. The greatest contribution of Schweitzer to the christological problem was his monumental *Quest of the Historical Jesus*,

which effectively demonstrated Jesus' eschatological pre-occupations if it did not discover the answer to the riddle of his self-consciousness in relation to the Messiah images familiar to him. He traced the development of the quest of the historical Jesus over the last century and ended on a somewhat wistful note, already quoted, which made clear that for him the historical Jesus was still the Christ.

Account must also be taken of the towering figure of Paul Tillich. A refugee from Germany, in his very person was imported to America the quality of German scholarship and first-hand acquaintance with the various theological movements current in twentieth-century Germany. Tillich, on the other hand, was no man's copy, as William Penn said of George Fox. He combined strains from various sources in a wholly original way. There was something of the Barthian "totally other" emphasis on the transcendental. At the same time, there was implied the mystical sense of immanence in the famous definition, "God is the ground of our being." But while he did not reject the historical nor the psychological, he held that God is known only by revelation apprehended by faith, an approach which places him more among the orthodox or neo-orthodox than among the mystics.

Meantime, in this century, there has been a succession of independent researchers into mysticism, who arrived at an extraordinary degree of concurrence in their analysis as to what constitutes its essence. These include Baron Von Hügel, Evelyn Underhill, E. Herman, Dean Inge, Rufus Jones and Walter Stace. They all agree that mysticism has nothing inherently to do with the esoteric, the occult, extrasensory perception, spiritualism, hearing voices or seeing visions, with all of which it is often confused. The most that can be said is that mystics are sometimes persons who are also psychics and experience some of these psychic phenomena, though they are usually wary of evidence so gathered.

The core of the mystical experience is the apprehension of unity and the perception of relatedness. For the mystics the world is one. For the greatest of them, there is even a diaphany of the divine at the heart of matter itself. And, as we have been pointing out, mysticism is itself a form of empiricism. Faith is reached by a unique process of induction, namely, first-hand mystical experience. Rufus Jones defines mysticism as "the type of religion which puts the emphasis on immediate awareness of relation with God, as direct and intimate consciousness of the Divine Presence. It is religion in its most acute, intense, and living stage."[2]

This is not to say that there have been no vagaries and aberrations in the history of the mystic way. Walking this narrow way, some have fallen over the precipice into neurotic and even psychotic behavior, as Rufus Jones and other researchers have conceded. But these excesses do not discredit the wholesomeness and spiritual health of the greatest of the mystics.

When dogmatists and ritualists experience a shaking of the foundations with reference to new world-views, the mystics are likely to remain secure and unperturbed. The evolutionary and depth-psychological perspectives can be taken in stride, confirming what had been "known" all along. Moreover, the new emphasis on the social gospel is likely to be embraced by the mystics as an inevitable consequence of the cultivation of the inner life. The mystical experience of identification with others is the surest sustained motivation for social action, the only insurance against the besetting temptation of growing weary in well-doing. It is no accident that Gandhi and Martin Luther King, Jr., had highly cultivated mystical faculties.

My own conviction is that the greatest influence on American theological thought within the last two decades

---

[2] Rufus Jones, *Quakerism: A Spiritual Movement* (reprinted by Philadelphia Yearly Meeting, 1963), p. 57.

has been exercised by two great contemporary mystics, Martin Buber and Pierre Teilhard de Chardin. That a Jew should have had so profound an effect on Christian theology is symbolic of the process of convergence in the noosphere, or thought membrane, encircling the earth. His interpretation of the presence of God in the event, "here where one stands," and in the heart of genuine dialogue, or meeting between man and man, has had a profound influence on Christian theology.

Teilhard de Chardin, whose books have become generally known and read only in the last decade, has had an extraordinary effect on Catholic and Protestant theology alike. Perhaps he is one of those mighty creative geniuses to whom Albert Schweitzer looked as one who would chart a new course in the understanding between history and theology. In any case, not since Paul has there been a new Christology of such cosmic dimensions. The Point Omega toward which the whole evolutionary process tends is the Christification of the universe.

Teilhard's enthusiasm, it seems to me, should be tamed by the sobering fact of recurring extinctions of whole species within the process, due to overspecialization. I also believe that in some respects he did not arrive at conclusions that would seem to have been indicated by the direction to which he committed himself. For example, I would have thought that no place remained within Teilhard's system for a virgin birth or a flesh-and-bones resurrection. Yet to my knowledge he nowhere renounces a literal interpretation of these doctrines. Further, it seems to me that his terms "divinization" and "hominization," with reference to man's continuing evolution, do invite dialogue with other living religions, whereas "Christification," unless it be carefully detached as a process from the Jesus of history, tends to preclude dialogue.

One conclusion reached by Teilhard in his study of evolution has peculiar relevance for us at this point. Whereas until recently man's evolution has been marked by dispersion and separate development, henceforth it will be characterized by convergence and integration. This of course will apply to the entire noosphere and will include an intensifying of interaction between cultures, ideologies, and religions. Already we have noted in America a great increase in public interest in the Eastern religions and evidence of syncretistic movements reflecting mutual influence upon each other of living religions to a degree never before experienced. Arnold Toynbee suggested some years ago that the world religion of the future will not be an artificial synthesis of existing religions. Organic continuity within history is vital to the health of any religion. Rather, that religion will prevail which shows itself capable of convincing those of other religions that nothing precious to them will be lost if they were to embrace the new faith.

Toynbee expressed the hope that the universal religion of the future might be some form of Christianity. I share this hope. Therefore my special concern is that we distinguish between the Jesus of history and the evolving Christ myth and that we seek some viable form of the myth that will draw a circle large enough to take others in. The general outline of such a Christ myth for modern man I now propose to offer.

V

The impending resurrection of the christ myth for modern man

In this swift survey of the historical evolution of the various strands of the Christ myth, we have seen how contemporary world-views in each period have affected this evolution. The underlying principle at work is the imperious demand of the religious impulse in man to bind into one bundle his experience and his expanding knowledge of himself and the world about him. One of the inexorable laws of life may be expressed thus: assimilate or perish. This applies in the realm of theological speculation, as in every other area. What cannot be assimilated into a contemporary world-view which has been informed by man's recently acquired knowledge of the facts of evolution and of depth psychology must be questioned, even if it be ancient and revered concepts of the Christ myth. Only that new form of the ancient myth may be retained whose lines succeed in following the curve of these new perspectives which characterize the modern mind.

The Need for a New Christ Myth

It is true that in our contemporary world, especially in America, we observe side by side religious groups in which the Christ myth has been preserved in primitive form as well as other groups in which the evolving myth has either been abandoned or radically transformed. It also seems possible for some minds to preserve airtight compartments, accepting in one area on authority or by "a leap of faith," on more or less literal terms, an orthodox form of the Christ myth, and adopting in another the inductive method of scientific reasoning. I do not want even to appear to stand in judgment on others. I am simply maintaining that if we are to win for the Church young men and women whose expanding world-view has assimilated the evolutionary and depth-psychological perspectives, and who are religiously motivated to keep their world one, we shall have to present to them a new version of the Christ myth which can be assimilated into their world-view. This is the grave responsibility of that branch of theology which has always been known as "apologetics": justifying the ways of God to man in order to win man's response to God in every new age.

We have seen in particular how prevailing philosophical and psychological currents have always influenced christological developments. The discoveries of the fact of evolution and of the duplex psychological nature of man have had an enormous influence on contemporary philosophy and psychology. A transformation on the scale of a revolution took place in the natural sciences as a result of the discovery of the process of evolution. This transformation of course was reflected in the new scientific discipline of psychology. The underlying assumptions of various schools of philosophy were also changed. The schools of materialism, evolutionism, pragmatism, naturalism, positivism, and phenomenology all represent basic reorientations in philosophy. We have noted that after the Middle Ages, philosophy generally rejected the role of handmaiden to theology. Indeed, in some circles a philosophy of religion began to supplant the discipline of theology. Theology became almost a handmaiden to philosophy, a reversal of the earlier dictum.

But some philosophies, which remained attentive to religious experience, retained an element of idealism and made plausible place, if more limited than heretofore, for religion, as in the philosophies of Kant and Hegel. Meantime a group of naturalists retained in their philosophical systems a place for the concept of God, notably Alfred North Whitehead and his disciple Charles Hartshorne, with his so-called theistic naturalism or naturalistic theism. The old conflict between realism and nominalism has had its modern counterpart but the categories have changed in name and connotation and might now better be described by the names idealism and realism, new forms, perhaps, of Aristotelianism and Platonism. Whatever the contemporary school of philosophy, if it is to hold respect in its own field, it must ask ultimate questions rather than proceed from unchallenged presuppositions. The tour-de-force achieved by Scholasticism was possible only until modern times.

Important as philosophy has always been in establishing a context within which theology articulates its doctrines, for both philosophy and theology in modern times the controlling complex of ideas has been modern science. It has been a case of both philosophy and theology having to assimilate revelations in the field of science, rather than the reverse. It is an age of science rather than of philosophy or theology. The criterion of whether any individual philosophy or theology is able to retain the respect of colleagues in other disciplines in institutions of learning has been whether or not it has proved itself capable of coming to creative terms with the nature of the universe science has been revealing to the modern mind.

The most relevant of these revelations have been, as we have argued, the evolutionary process and the depth-psychological structure of the human being. We ask now how the Christ myth can be trued up to this new plumb-line that has been lowered as a result of these "recently" revealed truths. Is there any form of the myth that can be embraced by the modern mind with the enthusiasm and the integrity that characterized the faith of the Middle Ages? Presently we shall consider what modifications of the six great christological doctrines of the Church would be required for any viable contemporary form of the myth by the standards we have set. We are referring to the doctrines of the preexistence of Christ, the incarnation, the relation between the two natures, the resurrection, the atonement and the second coming. But first we must make some general observations about the specifications required for any new model.

The Specifications for a New Model

The postscientific world is clearly not the same world as the prescientific world. We no longer contemplate a static universe of abiding essences, or forms and substances, such as Platonic and Aristotelian philosophy dealt with. We behold a dynamic, evolving universe in which, if essences, or forms, have any objective existence at all they, too, must be evolving. What is the essence of man: what he was in his progenitors ten million years ago, what he is now, or what he has it in him to become ten million years hence? Our universe is not a finished creation. It represents a continuing creation. Philosophically it may be possible to hold that all change and adaptation are random and fortuitous. But we are increasingly aware that there are established rules of the game in which the continuing evolution of life as well as matter takes place.

We recognize the presence of a potential, a "within-ness," which unfolds and materializes as it is drawn forth by the ever changing ecological environment. What or who was responsible for establishing the rules and implanting the potential of the "within-ness"? Whatever or whoever the author of the process, we are all present at this continuing creation. Clearly we have the opportunity of being co-creators in however limited a sphere. And, as modern men, we can no longer see anything, not even ourselves, save under the aspect of biological space-time, or duration. Evolution is the master fact to which any Christ myth will have to conform, the curve which its new lines must follow.

The ancient psychology of Plato spoke of the soul and of reason as eternal forms which were fused with body at birth in the making of a man. Much of modern psychology by strange irony has denied its ancient counterpart, professing that it knows nothing of a soul or "psyche" in the Platonic sense. It knows only the present psychosomatic entity that constitutes a man during his brief existence upon this earth. It does witness powerfully to the incredible and inviolable unity of personality or personhood. Nothing happens anywhere within this being that is not reflected throughout, whether the stimulus be psychological or physiological. It recognizes that the person is duplex, no longer simplex, as once was thought. There is the vast sphere of the unconscious, more complex and extensive than the conscious. And the Jungian school points to evidences of the existence of a collective unconscious in which may be stored racial memories and projections known as archetypal images.

If the criterion of advance in evolution is ever higher forms of consciousness responding to ever more elements in the total environment, then one may well look to the unconscious for the promise of emerging forms of consciousness. The unconscious may contain the "within-ness" which may take conscious form in the future. It may be capable of revealing to man the new man he has it in him to become. Indeed the unconscious may be in the most profound sense itself the ultimate source of the Christ myth. The Christ myth as the image of the perfect man may reflect a revelation derived from the unconscious of the "within-ness" of man, the potential for the new man. All we know of God springs from projection of the very best values and attributes we experience in embryo in man himself. These values and attributes discovered in partial and fragmentary form in man we expand in imagination and project upon a hypothetical being, God. What we find "writ small" in man we assume dwells somewhere in this vast universe "writ large." But we have no other place to begin our quest than man himself. William Blake understood this:

> Thou art a man.
> God is no more
> Thine own humanity
> Learn to adore.

Our concept of God is inevitably and incurably anthropomorphic. We assume that if there be a God he must be Jesus-like because Jesus reflected the archetypal image of the Christ myth of perfect manhood that has always preceded unconsciously our images of the attributes of God. The realization and acknowledgment of this fact may initially be difficult for us, for we have been taught from childhood that this transcendent God has revealed himself in a succession of mighty acts performed as miracles in an exterior way, supernatural interventions in history, including preeminently the great act of coming himself through miraculous birth in Jesus of Nazareth.

We thought that biblical times were different from our own, that our biblical forebears knew something we can not know. It is a very sobering but salutary insight to acknowledge now that men have never at any time had a clue as to the existence and nature of God save on the evidence of a presence experienced in themselves and in other men, to be distinguished from themselves and from other men. The crux of this observation is that this is all Jesus himself had to go on, and this is all the disciples had, except that they had the incomparable advantage of seeing this presence in and just the other side of Jesus the man.

It is also a sobering insight to reflect that both our idea of God and our Christ idea, our God myth and our Christ myth, for all we *know* may spring only from an irresistible longing in the depths of man's psyche. He may be projecting upon his universe the perfect man, Christ, and also the perfect being, God, with appropriately superhuman powers of omniscience, omnipotence, moral perfection, infinite compassion and agapé—love. If that is so, we should still, of course, have to inquire what or who implanted this haunting dream deep within us.

We have observed before that there has always been an equivalent in other religions and cultures of a Christ myth, whether it took the form of "the way" in Lao-tzu, the Bodhisattva or the Quetzalcoatl myth, etc.

We have recognized that within Judaism the Messiah myth developed with reference to the incredibly potent psychological need for the recovery of nationhood under a king in the Davidic line. Jesus pondered various forms of this already evolving myth, including the Son of Man form. Clearly he chose the Son of Man over the Son of David image as more accurately describing what might be looked for in the coming of the kingdom in the last days. To what extent, if any, he may have identified himself with the coming Son of Man is a question which, in all probability, we shall never be able to resolve. That his disciples made the identification after the resurrection experience with both images, in varying degrees, is quite clear. The Apostolic Church then proceeded to extend the identification to include also the Logos image and evolved the preexistence doctrine. The early church wrestled with the problem of the relationship in Jesus between the divine Logos and the humanity. Subsequently the Church has continued to project upon the historic figure the evolving archetypal image of the perfect man, the Godlike man.

What we have attempted to demonstrate is that the Christ myth as an evolving idea has had a distinguishable history of its own, beginning long before Jesus was born and continuing ever since, as well as having counterparts in other religions as comparable archetypal images arose and were attached to (became incarnate in) other historical figures. The Jesus of history was such a man as could plausibly bear the weight of the Son of David (in sublimated form) and the Son of Man and suffering servant images and could even assume, credibly, the burden of the Logos image and all the attributes of perfection that have since been foisted upon him by varying forms of Christian piety.

It is, of course, initially very difficult for us to train ourselves to distinguish between the Jesus of history and the Christ myth. But in the interest of the pursuit of truth we must learn to do so. This is not to say that we shall not continue to see personified in Jesus more than in any other historical figure all that we may now mean by the Christ as the perfect man, all of God that can take the form of a man. Indeed, it is my own conviction that the association of any viable Christ myth for our time must be primarily with the Jesus of history for those of us who have perceived the Christ in him more than anywhere else.

But at the same time it is important for us to see and to acknowledge that this emerging, evolving image of the Godlike man is not to be contained in or fully identified with that historical figure. The Christ image is to be identified with the indwelling Holy Spirit. In any Spirit-filled man or woman we perceive, however limited, the Christ figure. Jesus was a man. But the indwelling Christ is neither man nor woman and may be equally present in man or woman. So, inadvertently, our new version of the myth meets another specification by many women of our time: that we alleviate the oppressive "maleness" of our Protestant images of deity. Even in ourselves, so far as there has taken place the noble birth of the life of the Spirit, we recognize in this same "Aristocrat" the unmistakable family likeness of the Christ-life.

All this requires of us important distinctions we may not heretofore have been accustomed to making. We will not call *Jesus* good, as he himself admonished us. We will call the Christ-life (the way, the truth, and the life) we perceive in the biblical portrait good. We will not worship the Jesus of history as I believe he also would have counseled, had he foreseen what we have done. We will worship only that God to whom the Christ myth points, that God to whom the indwelling Holy Spirit witnesses. This Jesus of history was fully man. I believe that the divine indwelt him in greater unity with the humanity, more transparently, than any other man who has ever lived. But the divine also indwells us. We are all sons of God and sons of Man. The Christ within Jesus is the same Christ within us, but released in him for richer, more abundant life. This Christ-life is "the Royal Way of the Holy Cross." Nevertheless, the Christ-life can be born in me and in you in proportion as we are ready to respond and be obedient to the same divine will. The same Holy Spirit is prepared to conceive the same Christ-life in us.

The Preexistence of Christ

In what sense can we still speak of the preexistence of Christ? I believe we can make full and continuing use of the Logos concept. In the beginning was the Word, and the Word was with God, and the Word was God. This is still a viable myth: the Word or the Logos as the wisdom of God. We postulate an eternal God whose existence marks the beginning of time. "In the beginning, God." "In the beginning was the Word." The Word and God were one. It was through the Word that God created and still creates. The Word is God in his role of continuing creator. The Word is itself therefore uncreated. The Word is not even begotten of God. The Word *is* God. One may also say that the Word and the Holy Spirit are one. The Word and the Christ of the myth are also one insofar as the Christ of the myth is all of God one can put into the idea of a man, a God-man. But then God is no more for any man than the source and summation of the good, the beautiful, the true, the germ of which man has seen in himself and in other men, most fully in Jesus of Nazareth.

But we may not speak of Jesus of Nazareth as preexistent unless all men are preexistent. There is the hypothesis of the preexistence, as eternal forms, of individual souls. Plato's theory is as impossible to disprove as to prove. The ideas of transmigration and reincarnation have flourished for many centuries in the East and have increasing numbers of converts in the West. There are individuals who purport to have had intimations of earlier existence in other bodies and there are individuals who purport through various forms of clairvoyance to be able to tell others precisely what shape their earlier incarnations took. There are mediums who purport to be able to contact departed spirits and to communicate with them. There are many persons who have experienced interior separations from their physical bodies, and have beheld the Divine Light and other beings.

I trust that I may remain open to the possibility of some element of truth in all this, but as of now I remain unconvinced. It seems to me there remain other possible explanations of the alleged phenomena, including various kinds of unconscious thought-projection and wish-fulfillment. For our present purpose, the point we are making is that since Jesus was a man he could have had a preexistence only if the same is true for other men. It is one world and we are not to look for supernatural phenomena, only for natural phenomena, of many of which we may not as yet be aware. And we must remember, also, that, from the evolutionary perspective, if there are eternal forms we might call souls, these would be expected also to evolve and not merely to work out in successive migrations their *karma*.

From the same perspective we could also say, however, that insofar as the Christ-life is an emergent, at once quickening and justifying the Christ myth, this life has had a form of eternal preexistence in the "within-ness," the very womb of nature herself, by promise. The universe has from its inception been the kind of universe in which the Christ was always there by promise, even as life itself was asleep in matter before the arrival of a particular ecological environment, in the fullness of time, drew it forth, enabling some molecular substance to become cellular substance. It was not Jesus, then, who enjoyed preexistence, but the Christ potential which was incarnate in him and is to a lesser degree incarnate in all men.

This Christ potential and the Word are one, though we may postulate an eternal status for the Word, an existence outside of time, whereas man's conception of the Christ-life clearly evolves within time. This is the first way in which we must distinguish between the Jesus of history and the Christ myth. As far as we *know*, Jesus did not preexist the Nazarene. The Christ-life that came to flower in him did have a preexistence in the sense that this potential lay darkly hidden within the whole process by which life itself was first a possibility and then an actual-

ity on this planet, and may have its counterpart elsewhere
in the universe.

The Incarnation

What then of the incarnation, the basic doctrine of the
evolving Christ myth? The incarnation is not a phenomenon unique to Jesus. The Word, in some sense and in some
measure, is incarnate in all men. There was no need for a
miraculous birth to facilitate this incarnation. From the
evolutionary perspective the incarnation of the Word in
Jesus is vastly more wonderful and awe-inspiring. The entire evolutionary process has borne within its very bowels
the potential for this flowering of the Word in the man
Jesus from the beginning of time. Jesus is no freak. The
fulfillment of the Word in him was as natural as any other
phenomenon in nature, but of course for the rest of mankind the arrival of the second Adam is as stupendous and
portentous an event as the arrival through the evolutionary process of the first Adam, the progenitor of man.

Our Christology has to expand its horizons to encompass the breadth and scope of an incarnation whose
duration or process of becoming is as old as the very matter of this universe. There was no divine intervention. A
God who had once created the universe and called it good
as he set it spinning did not take another look aeons later
and in great anguish find that it had turned out very bad
in man. He was not called upon to set aside the ordinary
laws which had seemed good enough to keep things in
tow at its beginning in order to make a fresh and, hope-
fully, better beginning now by the intervention of divine
fiat. On the contrary, though the Christ in Jesus had been
a long time coming, as long a time as the age of the universe itself, if it could be said to have any age that could
be computed, here it was: a fresh occasion for celebration
in the same way as at the beginning, if we may still speak

metaphorically of any beginning. Behold, it was still very good!

And this incarnation in Jesus, while unique in degree, is not unique in kind. As Justin Martyr recognized very early, all men possess the Word incarnate. It has been imparted to the species, man, by the evolutionary process itself. It has been tenderly carried and cradled all the way up through the sap of life until it has borne this fruit in Jesus. All members of the species may celebrate this event in one of their number, because it points to a quality of life that resides by promise in the species, the potential for a new species, the new man. When some reptiles were in process of sprouting wings and becoming birds, other reptiles of the same species had no sentient capacity to apply the phenomenon to themselves, reflectively. But every man may look at the Jesus of history and say to himself: "The potential for this life-style, this royal way of the holy cross, also lives within me, however darkly overlain, blunted, and immobile."

I am drawn to revere this quality in Jesus because, in the first instance, there is that in me which has enabled me to recognize it and to affirm it. If I recognize and respond to this way of life as *the way*, even intermittently and often halfheartedly, my own self-respect is enormously enhanced. I have the basis in myself of a self-love the depth and magnitude of which I had never dreamed until now. Is that what a man can amount to? And I am a man! Now, no matter how great have been my failure and my sin, I am justified in entertaining hope. I can never justifiably hate myself again. In my own being lies the germ of the same potential, however frustrated and submerged. This incarnation in Christ is not a freak. It speaks to me of my own unlived Christ-life and calls it to birth. I can believe in the Christ myth because the Christ-life has been lived out here on earth as far as my mind is able to encompass it.

But I shall still have to distinguish between the Jesus of history and the evolving Christ myth. The man Jesus lived within time, subject to the limitations of time. He was born, had a brief lifespan, and died. His life was what it was. I can only know a little about it from the testimony of those who knew him in the flesh. But I must confess my conviction that as the Christ myth has continued to evolve from the resurrection experiences on, men have continued to impute to that life more than that life self-consciously experienced. That life has had a curious quality of elasticity in that it has seemed possible for it to expand in such a way as credibly to absorb the successive claims made for it. But in all honesty I must again recognize the difference between the life that was lived within the bounds of a particular place and time and the evolving Christ myth.

The two are not contiguous or identical, though they meet and commingle at many points. In the man Jesus there took place to a unique degree an incarnation of the Christ-life. But the incarnation is not "cribbed, cabined, nor confined" in that life. There have been many degrees of incarnation of the Holy Spirit, the Word, God, in many men, a supremely great one in Jesus, but the end of this process is not yet. We can say what has been and acclaim it with celebration. We are not gifted with the prophecy to proclaim what will yet be within this strange and wonderful process of which we are a part.

The Two Natures

For the first six centuries of Christian history there was endless debate over the two natures in Jesus. The orthodox position was (and has remained) that he was at the same time fully human and fully divine. Any position which stressed the one to the neglect of the other was adjudged heretical. Docetism was condemned because it underplayed the humanity, Arianism because it did not do justice to the divinity. But how these two natures were related to each other constituted a problem eliciting the imagination and forensic ability of the Church's greatest minds. We followed the arguments in outline in an earlier chapter. They centered around the question of whether the Logos constituted for Jesus the equivalent of the soul in other men which was fused with the flesh at birth or whether he had a human soul which became deified by association with the Logos. The latter attained the ascendency in an attempt to keep Jesus fully human, because the leverage of salvation seemed to demand it. There remained the other problem: having established the validity of both natures, how could they be integrated so that Jesus was one person? What was the nature of this union? Was it a commingling? Were the two natures juxtaposed, conjoined, indivisible, consubstantial? There was constant and heated debate. And though the last great ecumenical council at Chalcedon defined the tolerances, and the Church generally accepted these through the Middle Ages, after the Reformation there were new variations on old themes of dissent, as we have seen.

But the great divide on this issue came with the advance of modern scientific inquiry which occasioned whole new schemes of philosophy and psychology as well as theology. Thought no longer had to stay within the bounds of traditional dogma. Man was free to challenge any dogma with the two great modern touchstones of truth: reason and experience. The new inductive method made its imperious demands upon every discipline, including theology. This represented, as we have recognized, a full-scale revolution. There have been some all along who have managed to maintain two forms of thought process, one in religion and one for scientific inquiry. But this, we have maintained, is an unconscious betrayal of the religious impulse itself, which is *to put it all together*, to make it one world. Of course there are ways of knowing apart from the rational. But reason still is king. What it cannot retain as a plausible hypothesis must go.

The most recent of the relevant achievements of science by way of induction have been the discovery of the fact of evolution and the fact of an activity of the mind below the level of the conscious—now designated the unconscious. Both have a good deal to say to the historical assertions about the two natures in Jesus. In the first place, the very criterion of advance in evolution has always been ever more extraordinary unity within ever greater complexity. The human personality reflects the most remarkable psychosomatic unity of all. The maintenance of this unity in terms of identity and integrity is very precarious. Identity, as Emily Dickinson knew, is a hound that all too easily slips its leash. Nevertheless, when the person enjoys health of body and mind, there is sustained coherence and continuity of the elusive qualities of personality.

The development of the human personality, moreover, has emerged very gradually from evolving life in the direct ascent of man. It has been an unfolding from within in response to the changing environment. No new ingredient has ever been implanted from the outside. The implications of this are very important to our present inquiry. From the evolutionary perspective one does not look for, indeed cannot accept, an infusion from the outside at a particular juncture by a transcendent God. An indwelling from the very beginning of the potential for that tangible life-style that found expression in Jesus of Nazareth, yes! An incarnation of the Logos, the Word, the Idea, in molecular substance itself and all the way up through the evolution of cellular substance into the quality of divine life we recognize in Jesus, yes! But it is no longer possible for those of us who must true up our Christology to the perspective of biological space-time, or duration, to conceive of an exterior God choosing one individual within the species man and implanting in him in the place of a human soul, or infusing into that human soul, the divine Logos.

The Church has from time to time dealt with what it realized appeared to those on the outside a certain "scandal of particularity," a modern parody of which has been the doggerel "How odd of God to choose the Jews!" The Church has always made impressive defense. But from our modern evolutionary perspective the scandal of particularity has become quite intolerable. Particularity itself, yes! Have there not always been emergents? Has not significant particularity in the individual been the basis for the very origin of species, new species, always? Yes. But always the emergent particularity has been a drawing forth from within of a potentiality long buried, an ecological summoning forth of an interior promise in the shape of a new individual who could with other such individuals become the progenitors of a new species. Never an intervention from above or from outside which put to one side the due process of evolution itself! Despite the occasional freak in evolution, itself known scientifically as parthenogenesis, a virgin birth is out of the question. There is no need for it in a process which has been indwelt all along by the Logos. But even more there is no exterior transformation by divine fiat to create the "once only" God-man.

Here is no loss of mystery or wonder! I see it, rather, as an infinite enhancement of both, but redirected. Our response in awe and reverence is not to a numinous intervention in an otherwise mundane process. This response is now directed toward the diaphany of the divine present from time immemorial in the process itself. There is no supernatural superseding the natural. The entire process, including the new event in Jesus of Nazareth, is natural, but the natural is now seen in a new and pervasive way as indwelt by the divine.

It is one world, but this one world is inhabited by the infinite God who still shapes from within his expanding creation. He has at once a constant and a consistent milieu in which to work: nature. Spirit is ever emerging from within the unimaginable depths of matter itself. Jesus sprang from matter in response to environing matter through biological space-time. In him the holy of holies, the source and sustainer of the values man cherishes most, whom he has named the eternal God, was clearly perceived by a few other men. They did their best to tell us what they saw, and what they saw still quickens a like response in some of us. In this sense it is indeed the preached Christ that contains, as it was once the preaching Jesus who contained, the charisma that elicits the response of discipleship.

The most distinctive characteristic of the evolutionary process is assimilation, an ever more amazing integration between the inner potential and the nutritive elements drawn from the environment by interaction. Animals may be said to have a whole range of emotional and intellectual response but only one nature. This could be said to be an evolving nature, changing as varying species emerge. But at any one stage of development such is the remarkable degree of integration that one can speak only of one nature. This observation drawn from nature itself makes it impossible to conceive of two natures in Jesus.

Depth psychology bears the same testimony. Man could be said to have many selves in the sense of the demonstrable phenomena of autonomous complexes. There is also the presence of multiple disparate personalities in the psychotic man. All men experience what appear to be different "natures" in themselves, reflected in changing moods and dispositions. We are all hag-ridden by the threat of dissociation of these conflicting "natures." But the health of the person is manifest in one nature. Integration or integrity of the person is simultaneously the goal of psychiatry and of religion. It is simply impossible any longer to believe in and to attempt to interpret two separate and distinct natures in the man Jesus. He was all of one piece. It was not a case of a commingling of two natures, however intimate, within one person. In him there could have been only one nature, else he was some kind of freak or monster.

On the hypothesis of two natures in one person the modern mind, informed by the evolutionary perspective, inevitably conjures up some kind of Frankenstein or Janus. What we unforgettably learn from the insights of modern depth psychology is the marvelous unity of the human personality. Nothing can be happening on one level of man's being without inevitable reverberations and consequences on every other level. Chemical changes produce glandular changes, which in turn produce psychological changes, etc. Conscious experience and reflection make alterations in the content of the unconscious. Conscious behavior is affected by activity in the unconscious. It is both physiologically and psychologically impossible for any well person to have two separate and distinct natures.

So we can no longer speak of the two natures of Jesus. He cannot be said to be both human and divine if by divine something separate from, or antithetical to, the human is conceived. We can henceforth see him only as fully human. We can indeed perceive in him the divine, but only on the assumption that all men have in them the spark of the divine. We can believe in the incarnation of the Logos in Jesus of Nazareth, but only on the assumption that the Logos indwells in some degree all men. We may make a distinction of degree but not of kind. From the evolutionary point of view Jesus may indeed be a "sport," an emergent, a breakthrough of the new man, the second Adam. But this extraordinary phenomenon can be understood only as natural rather than supernatural.

There is no discontinuity, no intervention in the natural process by a God who stands apart from his creation and tinkers with it from the outside.

There are not two natures in Jesus, the human and the divine. There is one nature, the human, and in this one human being a divine element, present throughout the species, has burst into full bloom in the fullness of time. We may continue to identify the divine in Jesus as the Logos, the Word, the Holy Spirit. But we cannot confine the existence of the divine to this one man among men. Therefore we are not to worship the man Jesus, though we cannot refrain from worshiping the source of this Holy Spirit or Christ-life which for many of us has been revealed primarily in this historical figure.

The Resurrection

We shall speak of the resurrection before we come to reflect upon the atonement because the resurrection experiences historically preceded the theological doctrine of the atonement, although the atonement is associated with the cross as the manner of Jesus' death. We have said before that without the resurrection experiences there would have been no Church, no abiding promulgation of a Christ myth with reference to the Jesus of history. The disciples lived in a world in which recurrent manifestations of the supernatural as opposed to the natural were anticipated because they believed they could point to historical illustrations. Neighboring religions as well as Judaism had legends of resurrections. And there was the Lazarus story in which Jesus is himself said to have raised someone from the dead. The world-view of the disciples allowed for physical resurrection. At the same time, the resurrection experiences of the disciples created what dramatists would call the illusion of the first time. This was not just one more resurrection. Paul expressed the *sine qua non* aspect of the experience and the doctrine about it when he said, "If Christ be not risen from the dead, we are of all men the most miserable." There is no question but that the authors of the New Testament believed in a flesh-and-bones resurrection, logically related to an empty tomb. But can we accept the idea of a physical resurrection dependent on an empty tomb for verification?

Neither the evolutionary nor the depth-psychological perspective of modern man knows anything of the resurrection of the body in this sense. From the evolutionary perspective the physical resurrection of the body constitutes an insuperable obstacle to reason. There is no place, in a process in which permanent disintegration of the body is as essential to life as birth, for bodies that reassemble and rise again. Moreover, if a body is resurrected it thereafter presumably survives in eternity as it was here. At what stage of its earthly life: the peak of its development, or various stages of advanced decrepitude, or physical condition at death? Since evolution reigns here, can we conceive of a static life for a resurrected body hereafter? If the nature of the universe is to evolve, does a resurrected body evolve? The questions that the doctrine gives rise to preclude belief by the modern man.

Yet the resurrection experiences were germane to the founding of the early church. Do they then allow a different interpretation from the traditional flesh-and-bones, empty-tomb version, literally accepted? I believe they do. What the disciples must have experienced was a powerful awareness of the real presence of the Christ life they had perceived in him, so potent an awareness that naïvely but quite sincerely they unconsciously projected this presence into audio and visual impressions that bore every characteristic of objectivity. As suggested earlier, the resurrection experiences may have been partly occasioned by associations in the unconscious with a mystical experience at the time of baptism, if Morton Smith's interpretation of the "mystery of the kingdom" is considered acceptable. The experiences must nevertheless have been basically subjective.

This is not to say they were not genuine experiences that transformed despair into hope, desolation into confident assurance. There was enormous psychological need for reassurance. There may have been words of Jesus that spoke of his anticipated return to their midst. Something happened that convinced them he had returned. And there was even a time when these resurrection appearances ceased and people no longer looked for them. There was an experience of an ascension which also seems to have been understood in physical terms by the author of the book of Acts. Then there was the experience of Pentecost. The disciples believed that the promised Holy Spirit came and visited them, alighting on their heads as tongues of flame and causing them to speak in varying languages while being comprehended by others who could not normally understand speech other than their own.

I can only understand the resurrection experiences as a mystical awareness that the Christ, the Holy Spirit, the disciples had known in Jesus was now suddenly present in and just the other side of one another, as T. S. Eliot suggests in his allusion to the experience of the two disciples on the road to Emmaus in his poem, "Ash Wednesday." We cannot of course eliminate the possibility of audio-visual hallucination caused by enormous compulsive need for reassurance that their Lord still lived. Perhaps it was some subtle combination of the two. In any case it is clear that they believed him risen from the dead and in a physical form that would require an empty tomb. We need not conjecture about the empty tomb as to whether the body had been stolen or a mistake had been made as to its whereabouts. The simple truth is that the modern mind cannot see life steadily and see it whole and believe in the physical resurrection of the earthly body of Jesus.

At the same time the modern mind has its own continuing intimations of immortality which persuade many of us that something of the individual survives death. Yet every claim of establishing contact with "departed spirits" is, thus far, less than persuasive. The messages and purported converse seem often too banal to win enthusiastic belief or to be of a piece with that prophesied state in which the soul is supposed to go "from strength in strength in perfect service." I do not want to be closed-minded here and trust I shall remain open to possibilities I have not experienced. Yet I must report that my own conviction of the likelihood of some form of individual existence beyond death does not spring from the claims of mediums and those who believe they have contacted their departed beloved. It comes from the kind of experience one has of the presence of the beloved while she yet lives but is absent, and a like experience of nonmaterial, nonsensual at least, presence after death. Being present at the death of a loved one, it is easier to believe that something survives that moment of death than that such a moment marks transformation into total and permanent oblivion and nothingness.

Happily, Jesus is represented to have said while he still lived: "I am the resurrection and the life. He that believeth in me, though he were dead yet shall he live." This saying, authentic or not, I find profoundly moving and persuasive. There was that in Jesus which is not subject to death: the Logos, the Word. It took peculiar form in him, as it takes peculiar form in each one of us. This, I believe, cannot die, though what form of life it assumes and in what way it continues to evolve as that part of me which survives death I haven't the slightest idea. I believe that this would be a continuation of "the life which is hid with

Christ in God" here and now, while I yet live. To know another "in the things that are eternal" is to know in him that part of his individuality which will survive death. But, knowing and experiencing in myself and in others the infinitely intricate interrelation and interdependence of body and mind and spirit in one psyche, I cannot believe that a disembodied psyche could remain quite the same. Conjecture in this field I believe to be nonproductive. We are not given presently to know.

What we can hold onto in celebration is that the Spirit that was in Jesus is alive and operative two thousand years later. There was indisputable resurrection for that Spirit, whether its only incarnation is in the spirit of the believer or not. Moreover, there is something cumulative and evolving about this Spirit. Evil, on the other hand, however widespread its temporary hold on reality, has within it the seeds of its own destruction. What evil movement can be demonstrated to have survived two thousand years, and to be still accumulating strength? Good seems to progress to ever higher intensity of being, evil always to devolve into nonbeing.

One can even now experience the resurrection of the Christ-life in those who are today genuine disciples of Jesus. One can even now experience this in himself. This Christ-life is what survives and lives. Paul and John called us to the existential experience of death and resurrection by "being-in-Christ" and "being-in-God." In this sense I can repeat with passionate conviction, "I believe in the resurrection." There is yet another sense in which I believe in the resurrection. Caryl Houselander defined it for me when she said to her fellow Roman Catholics: "You have been taught to believe in the empty tomb. Don't do that. The tomb is empty. Christ is risen. Rather stand before some human derelict in whom the dead Christ still awaits resurrection!"

The Atonement

We must now consider the Church's doctrine of the atonement from our current perspective. We need first to recollect that the idea of the atonement is based on the myth of the fall. Life in the Garden of Eden had been paradise until the serpent beguiled Eve to eat of the fruit of the tree of the knowledge of good and evil. This act of disobedience springing from presumption and pride was responsible for Adam's fall. This is the original sin which all men have inherited. So runs the classic myth. There is no punishment for man that can fit the crime and therefore there is no way in which he can redeem himself. One theory of the atonement is that the devil had ever since held man captive. The death of God's only Son is, as it were, a ransom paid the devil by God to set man free. Another was the imagery of the offended judge. The righteousness of God has been outraged by the sin of Adam, and succeeding generations of men. No punishment that could be meted out by God to men could be sufficiently severe to make propitiation. Therefore, once again only the sacrifice of one totally innocent, namely Jesus, can serve to reinstate man. Others have held that the atonement, or at-one-ment, is accomplished through response to the moral example of Jesus. But this is a far more recent variant.

From the evolutionary point of view there could have been no first man and first woman living an idyllic life in a Garden of Eden. Indeed, God could not have created man *de novo*. Man has been a long time coming, as long as the evolutionary process since life began on this planet, indeed as long as the age of the universe itself, since the potential for his ultimate arrival has been contained in matter from the beginning. The condition of his animal forebears may seem sometimes to man a blessed state of innocence, but if the metaphor of eating of the fruit of the tree of the knowledge of good and evil is to symbolize the arrival of the sentient, reflective capacity in man which bestowed upon him the responsibility for moral decision, then for modern man this can only be viewed, not as a fall, but as a quantum leap forward! Does anyone really want to return to the presentient level of being? With all the anguish attached to moral decision, given even the besetting condition of the cleft will (the good that I want I do not and the evil that I do not want, that I do), would anyone conscientiously trade for the dignity imposed by moral responsibility unthinking instinctual behavior?

If we are to retain a myth of the fall it must obviously be radically reworked. I believe we must remythologize the fall to symbolize the ever repeated existential experience of falling to a lower level of life when one is clearly called to attain a higher level. Man is an animal who is called to live as a man. As Teilhard suggests, he is on his way to becoming fully "hominized," to becoming a man. He has it in him to become the new man, the second Adam. This requires of him sustained obedience to the moral imperative whose laws are written on his heart. This is another aspect of a "within-ness" to which man has only begun to awaken. He is called to be a moral being filled with compassion, and deliberately to cultivate in himself the mystical consciousness which has only begun to dawn in him. He is entirely right in projecting the values he has discovered in himself on the omnipotent and omniscient being he names "God." He hypothesizes the existence and attributes of a transcendent God from the immanent God he has known as a presence in himself and in other men.

Man finds himself in a perpetually fallen state with reference to the aspirations that dwell within him. There is no question but that he is helpless of himself, and stands in need of a Saviour. Moreover, to be constantly aware of being in a fallen state is a grievous experience, given the intensity of the aspiration in man at his best. Men can well afford to be compassionate toward other men when they behold in themselves the infinite pathos of this agonizing longing and the terrible frustration of repeated failure. Sin is basically the failure to become what one knows himself potentially to be. Martin Buber wrote that when he was asked what sin is, he knew instantly with reference to himself, but hadn't the slightest idea with reference to anyone else. Man may be judged only by that sin which he himself recognizes as a fall from the state into which he believes his own God has called him. Only so may we understand the fall, and the very experience of an interior fallen state is paradoxically the evidence of man's evolutionary breakthrough, a leap forward, a call "upward" into a higher state.

From this inescapable perspective how does one understand what was accomplished by the life and death of Jesus? In the first place, clearly, nothing is accomplished automatically by the death of Jesus on the cross either by way of ransom paid or justice appeased. Millions of men have willingly given their lives for others, and in terms of protracted suffering have no doubt endured still more. The efficacy of Jesus' life for the salvation of mankind cannot be viewed primarily in terms of the cross as the manner of his death. If the cross is to remain the primary symbol of salvation it must henceforward be remythologized as representing primarily the manner of his life," the Royal Way of the Holy Cross," the life-style of compassionate, redemptive suffering. "He learned obedience by the things he suffered." These included misunderstanding and rejection by those who had pretended to love him, even those who on one level did indeed love him but were neither able to understand nor to follow the burden of his message.

What happened from the evolutionary point of view

was that Jesus alone broke through to the new level of being to which all men of sensitivity and aspiration have felt themselves called, at least to some degree. How else can we now interpret Jesus' words: "You won't understand who I am unless the Holy Spirit in you reveals the secret." Yes, only those aware in themselves of the moral imperative to rise to that level of being are capable of confirming it when they see it. In one sense only those in whom the Christ-life has already dawned, however tentatively and partially, are able to recognize and to acclaim it by calling him who lives on this plane "Saviour."

Jesus will forever be my Saviour because he has enabled me to understand the meaning of a persistent longing within the depths of my own being. I see in him the Christ-life whose seed is deeply implanted in me and in all men, a life that has been unlived in such degree until Jesus came. I do not know when the world will see his "like" again, but I believe Paul's word, spoken in a different context and completely innocent of our evolutionary perspective, has by coincidence strange new relevance: Jesus is the first-born among many brethren. He is indeed the second Adam, the progenitor of a new race of men. If these brothers and sisters come at the infinitely patient pace of evolution, I doubt not that they *will* come!

The atonement is indeed the at-one-ment in the sense that Jesus has forever confirmed for me the reality and the value of the divine life buried deep within me. In some profound sense, when I look to him as "the way, the truth and the life" and strive to become his disciple, as long as I remain obedient or even in proportion as I achieve a partial obedience for, alas, so limited a time, I find that there is an at-one-ment interiorly experienced within me; that is, with my deepest "me," and with my God with whom at that level I am inextricably one.

Now I understand why Jesus experienced such exhilaration, almost a form of intoxication. He had happened on the secret of a new level of life, never before or since realized. Now I understand why he was driven to create one parable after another, and to enact some parables as in the triumphal entrance into Jerusalem, the cleansing of the Temple, the foot-washing ceremony, and the Last Supper, in order to convey to the only partially responsive disciples the quality of the new life. He seems to be saying: "When it comes to interpreting the kingdom as an already realized state of being as well as future event, I am the greatest. . . . Those of old time said unto you, but I say. . . . I know what I'm talking about. . . . I'm living in it. Look. It's like this. . . . It's like that. . . . Let the scales fall from your eyes and behold. . . . If you will follow me into the kingdom here and now, you will have life and have it more abundantly than you have ever dreamed." From the evolutionary perspective this way of life was its own reward. "Who for the joy that was set before him endured the cross." The incomparable joy of presently living in the kingdom! This *was* and made it possible to *celebrate* "the Royal Way of the Holy Cross."

We do Jesus a disservice to describe this way as a *via dolorosa*. Of course he shrank from the impending cross and prayed that the cup might pass from him. Of course those final steps on the way were a *via dolorosa*. But as an inevitable conclusion, within the context of the world in which he lived, for the life-style he had discovered he was able to accept it with equanimity. So utterly fulfilling had it been to live as he had lived!

"He needed not that any should testify of man to him, for he knew what was in man." He knew the depths of degradation and depravity. But he also knew as none other has ever known the ineffable beauty and goodness that had their home in man, if they could but be called forth. He was the light of men, all men. He showed them this beauty that dwelt within, despite the all but overpowering ugliness that also dwelt there. He showed them how it might find expression in a way of life. He demonstrated the present reward and fulfillment in pursuing this way. It was once said that he who teaches me of my meanings is master of all I am. Of course, then, he is my Master. How can it be otherwise? And on a scale the magnitude of which I had never dreamed, even on the scale of evolution itself. Clearly he is the new man whom man may evolve into, if he will. Is not one who shows me the way to go if I would find more abundant life my Saviour, if I have the will to follow as a disciple?

Of course he does not automatically save me. I must discover the will to follow within myself. But from my pathetically fallen condition he is my potential Saviour. He has taught me to find the Holy Spirit, the Christ-life, deep within myself. If the kingdom in which he habitually lived becomes for me the pearl of great price and I can be motivated to aspire unto it, he can show me how to take the first faltering steps.

The life which he lived and to which he bore witness is the Christ-life. This Christ-life is the life of God lived as a man. We have seen the Christ-life in Jesus as we have seen it in no other man. The Christ-life is the life of the Logos, of the Holy Spirit in man. To a far lesser degree it has been lived with infinite variation in other men, at least for seasons. The family portrait is to the life the same. The Christ, then, is the new man that is coming with all the patience of evolution to greet us in man himself. He is quite indistinguishable from the Holy Spirit. He came in Jesus preeminently, but he was not confined to Jesus and we will meet him partially and momentarily in other men and in ourselves. Because he lived fully and in a sustained manner in Jesus we shall always be able to recognize him in other men and in ourselves.

We can no longer accept the old Christ myth which identified the Christ with Jesus alone. This particular form of myth is dead for some of us. But there can be a resurrection of the great myth, a remythologizing that can infuse new life into it for men in our day. The Christ myth disengaged from the Jesus of history can continue to evolve so as to be viable for our new age. This disengagement can also enable other living religions to communicate with us about the Christ myth and its counterpart in their faiths. And we shall be able to share with them the Jesus of history, who was unacceptable to them so long as the Christ myth was held to be coterminus with Jesus' life on earth and beyond.

The Jesus of history, far from waning in our interest, as would inevitably be true for modern man otherwise, will, rather, recapture our interest and involvement. Seeing the Christ-life in evolutionary perspective we shall be drawn irresistibly to it where it has enjoyed its paramount incarnation in him. Because to live the Christ life is to enter the kingdom here and now we shall have to turn to Jesus again as disciples. The mystery and the beauty and the wonder will draw us as powerfully as ever they have. But we shall be able to look again at the historical figure without a divided mind produced by an image we can no longer make part of one world. Religion itself demands that we make our world one.

We shall be able to see now how the Christ myth is related, not only to the Holy Spirit perceived in the life of Jesus and to some extent in other men, but also to the archetypal image of perfect manhood which rises from the depths of the unconscious to meet us in dreams and fantasies. We should expect the Christ-life, involving a new form of consciousness, to break through from the unconscious which holds all the precious treasury of "within-ness" in man, the vast extent of which still remains largely unknown. We shall learn to be more attentive to the God who can best be known where he is nearest, deep within our own being. We shall learn, as P. T. Forsyth counseled us, to overhear the converse between the Father and the son in the illimitable depths of our own souls. There, guided by our Lord and Saviour, Jesus, we shall be led to meet the Christ.

Instead of a salvation history confined to the mighty acts recorded in the Bible, culminating in the life and death and resurrection of Jesus, our remythologized Christ myth will have to be expanded on an evolutionary scale. The fabulous narrative must take a form something like this:

God so loved the world that he implanted deep within matter itself the seed that in the course of his continuing creation through evolution would one day bear fruit as the Christ-life in Jesus of Nazareth, thereby winning other men to the discovery of the same seed in themselves, to the end that the new man might be born and the kingdom come on earth.

The Second Coming

Finally, in what sense may I believe in the traditional concept of the second coming of Christ? The hope first arose in the Apostolic Church when the disciples were confronted with the fact that the kingdom had not come while one whom they identified as the Messiah had been still with them in the flesh. It is clear that Jesus believed, as they did, in the eschatalogical coming of the kingdom as well as its present manifestation in his own life and potentially in that of others. When he saw that his own death would probably intervene before the coming of the eschatalogical kingdom, he may well have spoken of his return to join them at the heavenly banquet, as he is reported to have promised. Therefore the disciples may well have had his personal assurances of his second coming. But the failure of the final kingdom to arrive while he was yet present in the flesh made the second coming a psychological necessity for them. The resurrection experiences had also confirmed and deepened the faith.

Moreover, it is quite obvious that they expected the second coming, the parousia, to take place very soon and must in the earliest period have been somewhat preoccupied with this anticipation, a state of mind reflected in the synoptics and in Paul's early letters. Gradually, with the hope long deferred, there was occasion for counsel that they should get on with the business of living, for no one knew the time nor the season, and the kingdom might well come "as a thief in the night." It was important to be prepared for its coming lest one be caught off guard and in a state in which he would be rejected. But one was not to go about looking for its immediate coming, since it was not to be taken by storm.

Without abandoning the hope of the future kingdom, the author of the Gospel of John evolved a modulation of the hope into a present experience of a kind of realized eschatology in which those of the way might presently experience the kingdom in which Jesus himself had lived while on the earth. And the second coming, while objectively to be anticipated still in the future, could be experienced and appreciated, as often as the Holy Communion was partaken in spirit and in truth.

Now we stand nearly two thousand years away from the first coming, and there has been no second coming in the literal sense in which it was at first projected. There are still many Christians who await a literal second coming, as indeed there are many Jews who still await a first coming. But once again our new evolutionary perspective does not permit assimilation of this aspect of the classic myth into our contemporary world-view. Once again, remythologizing is essential, if we would retain any kind of continuity with the original faith. Here again, the first step toward embracement of a new, viable form of the myth is disengagement of the Jesus of history and the Christ or the Christ-life.

If the Christ is now to be understood as the image of

the new man, the Son of Man, man's successor, the second
Adam, whom we have beheld primarily in Jesus of Nazareth but have also caught glimpses of to a far lesser degree in other men, and even, in moments of mystical experience, in the depths of our own being, then of course
we shall look for innumerable second comings, of varying
intensity and fullness, as far as we can see into the future
and much further. But we shall no longer be able to look
for a second coming of Jesus of Nazareth, any more than
we shall look for the return to this earth of any other
historical figure or of anyone we have known and loved.

We shall of course be reticent about identifying specific
brothers of the first born. But all of us who accept this
idea of recognizing the family likeness of the elusive
Christ image would be able to build our own list of ava-
tars in this sense, both living and dead, in whom we have
been able to perceive elements of the Christ-life. Certainly in this sense we would have no difficulties with a
Black Christ, or a Brown or Red or Yellow Christ. But
with endless fascination we shall peer into every coun-
tenance of man, woman, or child for the reflection of what
Paul called the glory of God in the face of Jesus; and we
shall examine every life-style to catch the unmistakable
marks of "the Royal Way of the Holy Cross."

I shall expect the Christ-life we have known preeminently in Jesus to continue to emerge along the ever fleet-
ing frontier of living human beings in any given period
and at any inhabited corner of the earth. The Holy Spirit
has not left himself without witness at any time or place.
Strange, how well distributed on the face of the earth
have been men and women of the Spirit! Sometimes when
Jesus has been described to primitive peoples who have
not heard of him there has been the witness of *déja vu* by
one or more of them: "But I have known him!" The Christ
came in Jesus. He (if we be permitted a reluctant use of
the masculine pronoun) has come to some extent in others

and will continue to come. Every newborn babe bears promise of his coming. He will return again and again in many different persons. And in the course of aeons of time perhaps the image will change and evolve.

But I shall not look for him to come in miraculous birth or descending from the sky, trailing clouds of glory in some divine fiat at the hands of a transcendent God who stands apart from his created universe. This God is immanent in, as well as transcendent to, his creation; and he continues to create. He has placed hidden potentials within realized creatures and set in motion processes of interaction with environment in ecological interpenetration in which many wonderful revelations of being, as well as doing, are yet to take place. Jesus was no doubt right in his prophetic modesty: "Greater things than these shall ye see and do."

We will look for the Christ to emerge in a great apostolic succession of men and women until the kingdom comes on earth. That great tapesty that hangs above the high altar at Coventry Cathedral, in which some of us have seen what appears to be the Christ figure breaking through the very shell of evolution, as though the entire process had been like a mighty egg, incubated by the love of God until now—that is an unforgettable image of the depth and extent of the incarnation. From the evolutionary perspective it is inconceivable that such an incarnation should take place once and for all. We shall await the coming of the brothers and sisters and individually count them one by one in the secret places of our hearts.

More poignant still, we shall learn to look within the immaterial depths of our own being for the unmistakable archetypal image, preserved and harbored in our own unconscious, and await with infinite longing the noble birth in the life of our own souls.

Remythologized in conformity with the new perspective of evolution and depth psychology, we shall understand the incarnation as the fulfillment in Jesus of an annunciation proclaimed by the presence in life itself of this promise from its initiation on this planet. The fabulous narrative, an epic on the scale of evolution itself, now begins for us far earlier than we had ever dreamed. And, as in Yeats' poem, it concludes here, where one stands.

> And what rough beast, its hour come at last,
> Slouches toward Bethlehem to be born?

When shall we realize that the second coming may take place no further away than our own hearts, and say to ourselves: "I am myself the beast and I am Bethlehem. Can Christ be born again in me?"